How did it get so late so soon?
It's night before it's afternoon.
December is here before it's June.
My goodness how the time has flewn.
How did it get so late so soon?

- Dr. Seuss

THE COLLEGE FUNDING DILEMMA

LEARN THE SECRETS THAT WILL SAVE YOUR RETIREMENT

THE COLLEGE FUNDING DILEMMA

LEARN THE SECRETS THAT WILL SAVE YOUR RETIREMENT

By: Edward C. Vosganian

THE COLLEGE FUNDING DILEMMA

LEARN THE SECRETS THAT WILL SAVE YOUR RETIREMENT

ISBN: 978-1-7325893-4-6

Printed in the United States of America

Year of First Printing: 2020

FOREWORD

Do You Really Learn Anything in College?

Times are scary right now. Everything of value keeps going up in cost. Those people who believe inflation isn't a real thing should really pull their heads out of the sand. Some people believe one of the most valuable things you can acquire—that has immense value—is a college education.

Now, I am fully aware some kids go to college and waste their time and money. Also, some colleges may not even be worth paying for. And, some kids should go to a trade school that is suited to their skill.

All the same, as a college graduate myself, I can say I learned some very valuable skill sets in college. First off, I learned how to finish something I started. I learned how to read, write, think, and communicate more effectively. I may not remember every detail of every test I took … yet, I learned probably the most valuable skill set during my college years: how to solve problems.

Is that worth paying for? Absolutely. And the costs to acquire that skill are only going up. If you check the prices of attending college over the last twenty years, you almost feel sick to your stomach. Everything has gone up, from the cost of books and tuition to living expenses. Sadly, it doesn't appear to be coming down anytime soon.

This has caused some people to throw in the towel and think, "It's too expensive to attend college; I'm going to get a job and start working instead." Most hard-working families don't have the additional capital to pay $40,000, or higher, for one year of a college education. Some college costs, over the course of your time there, might put you into massive debt.

This makes it appear daunting to even try to get into those types of colleges if your standard of living may not support that. For others, it appears virtually impossible.

Not a surprise that some families have tried to cheat their way in. For those that didn't get caught, I guess luck was on their side. Others paid hefty fees for cheating and others served jail time. That's a high price to pay simply to see a child get into the best college. What has immense value will drive people to do some crazy and even illegal things.

So how does one overcome the impossible? Fortunately, there is a way, a proven process that's been around for a select few who were privy enough to find it. Ed Vosganian is one of the few who knows the secrets. He has personally helped thousands of families overcome this massive obstacle and achieve their dreams of acquiring a college education.

I would highly encourage you to listen to his words of wisdom. For those who feel like they know a better way … trek down that path at your own peril.

Want to see your (or your child's) dream come true?

Then listen to every word Ed speaks.

Ethan Kap
Inc. Magazine, Best Selling Author

Table of Contents

FOREWORD

Do You Really Learn Anything in College? 7

CHAPTER 1

How I Learned the Secrets of Getting into College Without Breaking the Bank... 13

CHAPTER 2

Why Parents Feel Like They Have to Cheat the System 29

CHAPTER 3

You've Been Lied to ... Top Ten College Planning Myths 37

CHAPTER 4

The Truth About College and Retirement: What You Don't Know Now Could Cost You Thousands of Dollars Later 51

CHAPTER 5

Don't Fall for Student Loan and Scholarship Scams 65

CHAPTER 6
HOW THE IRS CAN HELP PAY FOR COLLEGE 75

CHAPTER 7
HOW TO GET THE FIRST TWO YEARS OF COLLEGE FOR FREE 95

CHAPTER 8
CHOOSING THE RIGHT COLLEGE 113

CHAPTER 9
PAYING FOR COLLEGE 139

CHAPTER 10
ADMISSIONS AND FINANCIAL AID REALITIES 155

CHAPTER 1

How I Learned the Secrets of Getting into College Without Breaking the Bank...

As you may have noticed there's a trend in college planning lately— parents these days are going to great lengths to get their children into college and are risking more than their savings to do it. It isn't uncommon for parents to overreach to make sure that their child gets into a good school, but some have even gone so far as to sacrifice their retirement. Part of what is driving some of this behavior is the fact that most families aren't having real conversations about the landscape of college planning, and how hard it has gotten to pay for college.

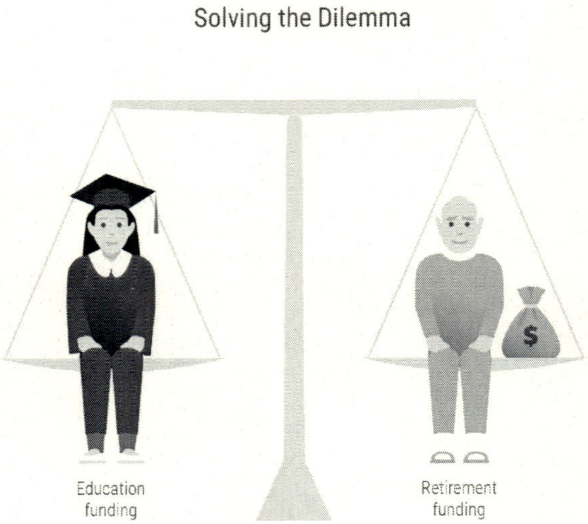

How can I determine the most suitable way to fund college and retirement?

Before we get into why college is so expensive—and why that trend is only increasing—let me tell you a little about how I got into the college planning business.

I was one of the lucky ones, I got to go to college before this trend started happening. Like most parents, my mother and father did their best to set me up to succeed—unfortunately they weren't rich, so I had to figure it out for myself.

I grew up in Farmington Hills, Michigan, a middle class suburb of Detroit. My dad was head of corporate investments for a major U.S. Defense company, and my mom was an elementary school teacher. My childhood was filled with memories of watching sports with my dad and waking up early to run my paper route—but it felt like all of that came to an end in the spring of 1990, when financial troubles hit our family.

On November 9th, 1989, we sat around the TV and watched in amazement as the Berlin Wall fell. I was a Sophomore in high school, just fifteen years old. As Communism's grip on Eastern Europe crumbled, we had no idea how the events we saw on the screen that night would come to affect our family.

The Cold War finally ended, and the U.S. Government began to reduce its wartime spending. This sent waves of layoffs throughout the U.S. Defense industry and my dad was one of the many casualties. Six months later, he came home with a pink slip, he'd lost his job. Because of his age—he was fifty-nine—it was hard to find employment. He got a few odd jobs here and there, just to bring in some extra money, but eventually, he decided to retire, and my family went from two incomes to one. Times were tight, but luckily, we stayed in our home.

By the time I was seventeen years old, I was already thinking about where I wanted to go to college. I also knew I would have to pay for it myself. Both my parents had gone to college and the value of education was passed onto me and my sisters. Even if it was a community college, I was expected to go.

At the time, I had two older sisters in college. I guess you could say we were a "Michigan State family," but MSU was my second choice, actually. I wanted to major in Marketing, and while MSU had a great business school, my mind was set on where I really wanted to go: UCLA.

I had big dreams of living in Los Angeles, going to school, and spending my weekends at the beach.

We were sitting at the dinner table one night when I told my parents I wanted to go to UCLA.

My parents looked at each other and said, "No way."

Here's why: Los Angeles was too far away, and UCLA was too expensive. Most of the money was going to their mortgage, so it was pretty much all on me. Plus, they wanted me close by, and MSU was only a short drive away. So, I filed my California dreams away, and enrolled at Michigan State.

Thankfully, I stayed open-minded to going to a less expensive college, because it could have been a financial nightmare.

Back then, I had no clue about the process, or the games people played to get into college, some of them were even illegal and unethical. We were also unaware of any Federal, State, or University aid to alleviate the stress of college costs. Even with my dad's job loss, we still felt we made too much money to qualify. Our belief was that you needed to be dirt poor or on food stamps before they would help, and because of that, we potentially lost thousands of dollars out of sheer ignorance.

So, I went to MSU and worked multiple jobs to pay for it. Luckily, I had some money saved up from working throughout high school unloading trucks and doing landscaping work, and I used it to cover some of my college costs.

But, funny story, I almost didn't make it to college...

It was the 4th of July during the summer of 1992, and I had just graduated high school and was getting ready to start classes in a couple months at Michigan State University. That day, a few of my buddies and I got together—we wanted to hang out, as we were all going to different schools in the fall and wouldn't be seeing each other as much.

We spent the whole afternoon hanging out. As evening fell, we headed over to a local shop to purchase a variety of fireworks to shoot off at a friend's house later. That night we set everything up on our friend's lawn and started firing up the fireworks stash we'd bought. One of my friends decided it would be hilarious if he lit one of the rockets and pointed it at me.

As soon as I saw him light the fuse, I ran as fast as I could to escape the incoming chaos. It was pitch black, so I had no idea I was running straight toward a large iron planter in the shape of a cauldron sitting in front of my friend's house. I ran full speed ahead, looking back over my shoulder, and slammed knee-first right into the object.

The rest was a blur, but they said I did a few flips in the air before I landed. The pain was unbearable. I remember lying there, convinced I had shattered my knee cap. Luckily, it was just a major cut, and all it needed were stitches in the emergency room and a few days in the hospital. After they released me, I went through a month of physical rehab, wore a knee brace, and used crutches, but I missed out on the 4th of July, and the rest of my summer.

Years later, I still have the scar on my knee to remind me of that day, plus my friends never let me forget (it's a popular topic of conversation, even today). But I look back on those three days I spent in the hospital and realize now how lucky I was.

During this time, I thought back to my grandfather, who had always instilled in me the need for education and hard work. He was born in 1911 in the Ottoman Empire (modern day Turkey) to Armenian parents. By 1915, under the guise of WWI, the Muslim Ottoman Turks had begun gathering up Christian Armenians and massacred over 1.5 million of them. After losing two brothers (one of which was his twin), my grandfather escaped to America with his mother and father at the age of seven. They immigrated to the United States, not only to escape persecution but also for a better life. They settled in Detroit, Michigan, and quickly assimilated into the community and learned English.

After a decade in the States, the Great Depression hit, and instead of going to college, my grandfather had to work. He owned a successful shoe repair and hat cleaning shop and later added a tailor shop to the business. During WWII, he got his realtor broker's license and ended up running a successful real estate company for the next fifty years. To this day, my grandfather's lessons have stayed with me. He always told us that with hard work and perseverance you can achieve your dreams and goals. And, of course, he insisted that his children and his grandchildren go to college. He wanted us to get the opportunity he never had, so we could go even further in life than he did.

My life could have been irrevocably changed in one moment. I thought to myself, *I was one of the lucky ones... I may not have gone to college at all.*

I realized that those of us who got a lucky break in life (and have guardian angels) have an obligation to lend a hand to others when needed. This might have been the first time I realized that I had a deep desire to help others. Naturally, this led me to start thinking about a career where I could be of service.

Like my father, I was interested in finance. After graduating with a degree in Marketing, a local company recruited me right out of college, and I decided to become a financial advisor. What I really wanted to do was help others grow and save their money. Since watching my parents struggle, I knew how life-changing this could be. But instead of focusing on retirement planning, like every other financial "guru" out there, I wanted to take it one step further. I knew how important education was, and I wanted to focus on college planning.

While I was learning the ropes and getting my licenses, I started noticing a pattern. There was a "college crisis" in America.

I realized that families weren't just having a retirement planning problem, but most were having a college planning problem as well, and the two were related. The more money they spent on college costs, the less went into their retirement accounts and savings. Many who were parents, around age forty to fifty-five, were struggling to get their kids into college, and it reminded me of my own parents. I wondered how things could have been different for us if we had proper college planning advice.

So, on my downtime at work, I started researching and learning the ins and outs of financial aid and the rules that were developed by the U.S. Department of Education. From scholarships to loans, I studied all the details. I realized my family had left thousands of dollars on the table because we were ill-informed.

In fact, I saw a lot of people were going about it the wrong way. Like my family, most families automatically assumed they made too much money for financial aid. Or maybe they thought they could get financial aid, but they didn't know where to start. They had gotten a little bit of advice, and filled out some forms, but they weren't really going through steps A to Z.

People just weren't educated, and many times parents missed out on great opportunities because of misinformation. As a result, many students are leaving college with too much debt, and are risking their retirement savings trying to pay off student loans well into their fifties and sixties. I came to the conclusion that in order to help my clients plan for retirement, I had to first help them plan for college.

Next to buying a home or saving for retirement, college is one of the most expensive things people ever do in life. And yet, nobody was out there educating parents on the path and helping them avoid the pitfalls of college planning. I had that knowledge, and I could help people save money and put more into their 401Ks and retire more comfortably because of it. And I knew that this niche market would give me an advantage over other financial planners. But the problem was that even after almost two years of working, I still wasn't making enough money to survive as a financial advisor. I was ready to quit.

I was living with my parents at the time, because I couldn't afford my own place. My job was 100 percent commission based, and I wasn't making much. I drove all over the metro Detroit area setting up at home appointments, explaining the college planning crisis to families, and that with the proper planning, how to avert it. It took a toll on me, all that drive time and long hours. I started having self-esteem issues, and my confidence suffered.

I started thinking I made a mistake choosing this field of work. Maybe I should just go work for "The Man." Get a nine to five, with benefits and a steady paycheck, instead of driving all over Southeastern Michigan having doors slammed in my face.

One day, I went down to the cafeteria in the building to have lunch with a couple other advisors.

I was feeling down, so I sat there pushing the food around my plate with my fork, not wanting to eat. I just wanted to go home and feel sorry for myself. One of the guys who sat in the cubicle next to mine was there and we were complaining about how much we hated our job.

Suddenly, in walked one of the most successful financial advisors in the company. This woman had been with the company a long time. She must have overheard us, because she walked right over to our table—and she looked at me and said, "What's wrong?"

I set the fork down. "I'm not making any money and I'm not helping people," I said. I told her I was thinking about getting out of the business and finding a nine to five job with a steady paycheck. No commission anymore, just a salary based job.

Her voice was quiet, but confident. She said, "Do you want to be told what to do every day with a boss breathing down your neck and hating your job? Or do you want financial freedom, with hard work and dedication, where you're the boss?"

Her words hit me like a bolt of lightning and made me sit up straight. I was listening.

She knew what I was focused on as an advisor, and in fact, she'd helped many of her own clients with their college planning save millions more for retirement. Then she made one statement that stuck with me and proved to be prophetic.

"If you can survive in this business for two years, you will be a lifer."

She knew I would be okay, at a time when I couldn't see it in myself. She was telling me to stick it out. I just had to bust my butt for two years and I would see the light at the end of the tunnel. It was the pep talk I needed, and it got me excited. I thought—*I can do this.*

She was right. My first two years were tough (I made barely enough to survive), but in my third year my confidence in my services and in myself increased, and my income started taking off, too. My business started growing on its own as more and more clients referred me to their friends, and I started feeling like I was really making a difference in a lot of people's lives.

One day, a client who was also a friend of mine came to my office. He had three kids and he was trying to figure out how to pay for their college without breaking the bank. He and his wife were making good money, about $200k a year, but I had a hunch they would still qualify for help. So, I set out searching high and low to find grants and scholarships for them anyway. After going through the process with me, they ended up only paying a third of what they would have on their kids' college tuition if they hadn't consulted me. I realized at that point, I could help anyone.

Over the past two decades in this business, I've been able to help thousands of families around the country afford college. While I was definitely drawn to financial planning initially because of the freedom (I didn't want to be chained to a cubicle all day), what really keeps me going is helping people. Without that, I would have burned out long ago. I've seen the joy it brings families as I help them navigate the maze of college planning, and the thousands of dollars they save in college costs that helps them make their retirement dreams a reality. People can sense that I'm sincere about what I do. This is personal for me, because it's something my family struggled with, and I truly want to educate people.

That's why I'm writing this book. I want to change the way people look at college planning. Today, the game has much higher stakes, and I know that parents are going to need help sifting through all the information.

If you aren't living under a rock, you may have noticed stories circulating in the news lately about people scamming the college system. And it's no wonder, because college isn't getting any less cutthroat or expensive.

College is EXPENSIVE!

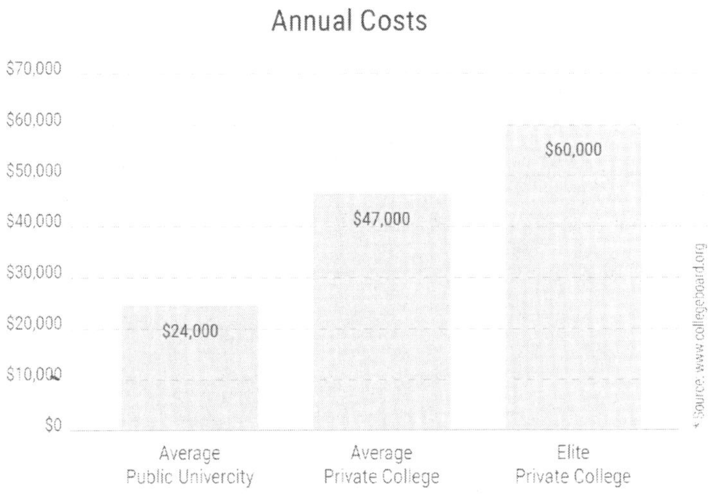

The average college tuition for four years, even for a public state school today is around $100,000, and for a private school, you're looking at $200,000 plus. Now multiply that by the number of kids in each family. Parents are either going into debt, or going paycheck to paycheck, trying to pay for it. Or the students come out with an insane amount of debt. It's no wonder politicians are talking about wiping out student loan debt or offering free college, or that there are even parents who think up elaborate schemes to cheat the system.

You don't have to do that. You don't have to go into debt, take out a second mortgage on your home, or rob a bank to get your kids into college. What most parents don't know is that there's literally billions of dollars out there. Colleges, just like any other business, don't want empty seats. You should never have to pay sticker price for tuition. There are ways to navigate the system without doing anything immoral—and I'm going to show you how.

Research of Parents' Biggest Concerns

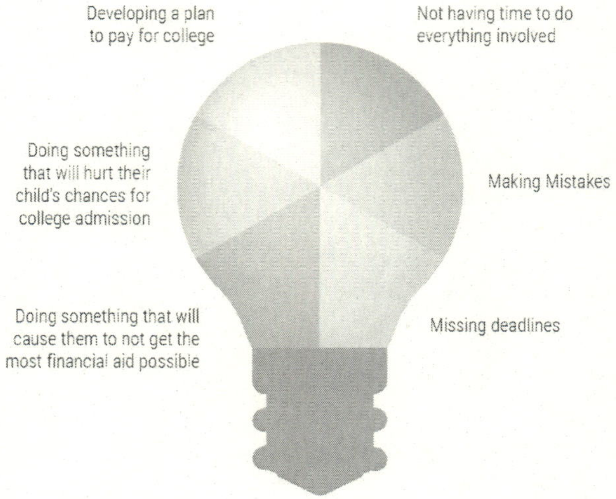

It took me many years to master college planning and I've learned a lot of secrets along the way. This book will help you navigate the financial aspects of college planning, ethically.

In the following chapters, I'll be sharing my unique process for college planning with you, using my database of knowledge, twenty plus years of experience, and my track record of success. This isn't some boring textbook on college planning you'd find on Amazon. You'll get real insider stories and information, not just things that are published everywhere on the internet. I will be providing case studies and proof along the way, so you'll know that the techniques work before you try them. We'll be covering everything from avoiding hidden costs, using the IRS to help pay for college, getting the first two years of college for free, choosing the right college, and the reality of financial aid and admissions.

It's really a one-stop-shop, so you can get a head start on the process.

Sure, you can do it alone (a lot of parents do), but it will take a lot of money and time, and you may make expensive mistakes. Even with hundreds of hours of research, there's no guarantee you'll be able to cut costs significantly. So, please try to suspend judgment as you read, you may be surprised at what you learn. Even if you think you're too late (or too early, for procrastinators), or you make too much money, or too little money, there's something valuable in this book for you. My whole goal with this book is to help you get your children through college without losing your sanity, your retirement savings, or winding up behind bars trying to pay for it.

CHAPTER 2

Why Parents Feel Like They Have to Cheat the System

I remember reading the headline in the morning newspaper: "COLLEGE SCAM."

For months it was all over the media, the famous "Operation Varsity Blues" case where dozens of rich parents got caught bribing coaches at prestigious universities to get their kids classified as star athletic recruits and illegally influence admissions. With eleven universities involved, fifty or more people named in the case, and over $25 million paid in bribes, it was the largest college bribery scandal in American history.

As a college planner, all I could think was ... *isn't it always that way? The ones who can afford it are the ones trying to cheat.*

> We joke about it, but there's always been an assumption (at least in America) that if you have enough money, you can buy your way into anything.

We joke about it, but there's always been an assumption (at least in America) that if you have enough money, you can buy your way into anything. Even Rodney Dangerfield wrote a big check to get himself back into college in the 80s comedy movie *Back to School*. Just recently, music mogul Dr. Dre famously donated $70 million dollars and put his name on a new building at the university (USC) where his daughter is now attending. This isn't new, it's been going on forever.

If those parents had been my clients, I would have simply told them—don't do it! It's not worth the risk.

There are a lot of opportunities out there, and there's a lot of great schools. You don't have to cheat to get your kids into them.

Unfortunately, they weren't my clients, and now they're paying millions more in legal fees and penalties than they would have originally paid in tuition had they done it the legal and ethical way—not to mention the potential jail time (maximum of twenty years in prison) they're facing.

Every day I see parents in all types of financial situations. Some who could afford to slap their name on a university building, and others who are just struggling to put one child through college without going bankrupt. In every case, I have always been able to find a way to accomplish their goals, without breaking the bank or doing anything illegal.

So, why do parents try to scam the system?

Some would say it's an image thing. Many parents are just "keeping up with the Joneses," they want to be able to boast that their son or daughter went to USC, or an Ivy League University. Admissions aren't guaranteed, and maybe some parents aren't confident in their child's abilities.

No, it's not your imagination, colleges have become extremely competitive and cutthroat. It's getting tougher and tougher for parents and students to navigate the college system. Not to mention college is expensive. In fact, the cost of tuition is going up faster than inflation, with some colleges raising tuition at a rate of 6 percent to 7 percent per year. According to statistics compiled by the U.S. Department of Education, as of Sept. 30, 2018: the average four year university student is leaving college with a student loan debt of $33,310. According to Forbes, it's a $1.5 trillion dollar crisis.

The $70,000+ Mark!

Cost of Attendance for 2019-20 Academic Year

1. $75,003 Harvey Mudd College
2. $74,580 University of Chicago
3. $74,001 Columbia University
4. $72,257 Barnard College
5. $71,956 Scripps College
6. $71,660 Trinity College
7. $71,620 University of Southern California
8. $71,392 Oberlin College
9. $71,338 Southern Methodist University
10. $71,270 Sarah Lawrence College

* Source: statista.com

As a result, some parents are going to extreme measures to avoid paying sticker price for college tuition. The other day I read about a case where a wealthy couple in Illinois were "divorcing" their children so they could apply for financial aid and need-based scholarships. These parents are actually going through the court system to surrender guardianship of their children to a family member in a lower income bracket, so they can pay less for college. This has been going on for years but is only coming to light in the public now.

Why Is College So Ridiculously Expensive?

- Less aid from government sources
- Teachers' salaries are going up
- Costs of maintenance, upkeep, repairs and infrastructure are going up
- Changes in technology
- Each year, college costs are increasing faster than inflation rates

So, why is college so expensive? Well, there's a variety of factors.

Inflation is partly to blame for this, also professors' salaries, and the simple fact that colleges are competitive. They need to compete with other colleges to get students into their school. That means shelling out millions each year on technology upgrades, modern facilities, sports equipment (especially if they're a big basketball or football school), etc. In other words, it's a "money thing."

To compound this "college crisis," admissions guidelines aren't always clear or transparent. This leaves parents feeling even more uncertain about their ability to get their kids into top colleges. Arbitrary rules are often applied as colleges decide which students get admitted and which don't. This is likely to get much worse with things like the "adversity score" that some colleges are rolling out, which will bump students perceived as coming from disadvantaged backgrounds into slots that could have been occupied by other students who are perceived as being privileged. So, if you've put in the hard work so that your children can have advantages in life, those advantages may be taken away.

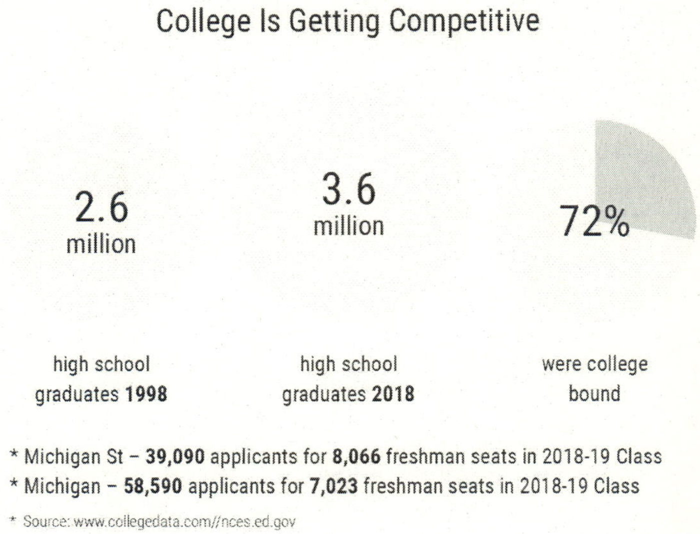

College in America is in a crisis. No, it's not really fair. But, in an unfair system, cheaters will still lose, and those with creative solutions will thrive. And there are ways to get your children into the best schools without going bankrupt or breaking the law.

Some of you might be thinking … why shouldn't I cheat? Shouldn't college be free, anyway?

If you have been listening to some politicians, "free college" is definitely a phrase that has been thrown around a lot lately. Even if you do believe that a college education is a basic human right, first of all, nothing is free. Someone is going to have to pay for it, and that usually means the taxpayers (that's you and me). Secondly, I'm not discounting it entirely, but I don't think we'll get there anytime soon. So, I wouldn't count on tuition going down in your lifetime, and I wouldn't hold your breath for "free" college.

So, what can you do to balance out the unfairness?

For starters, you can keep an open mind. If you're flexible, your tuition could be half the cost or more, and it'll still be a great school. The more open you are, the more opportunities you'll have. Unfortunately, parents tend to think the opposite is true.

I see parents make this mistake all the time, they only have one school in mind and no alternatives. Like the "Varsity Blues" parents, they are only focused on expensive brand name Ivy League schools because of the "image."

For instance, I recently had a client whose son loved skiing. They lived here in Michigan and they were looking to send him to Kettering University in Flint. I eventually got them to consider another terrific engineering school in Colorado (Colorado School of Mines). He not only got to ski the entire four years, he also got a great education at half the cost.

Secondly, you have to start thinking about colleges as a business. Colleges aren't that complicated—it's just a business, and all businesses operate for profit and reputation. And being motivated by profit makes them vulnerable to smart strategies and negotiation.

Do you think if you walked into an auto dealership and got a quote on a vehicle, and then went across the street to a competitor for a quote, then back again to the first dealership you would be able to negotiate a better price? Of course. College is a lot like buying a vehicle. Don't pay sticker price!!

We'll talk more about the hands on techniques later in the book, but ideally, what you want to do is find a handful of good schools and get them to compete for your student.

And lastly, don't wait. So many parents put off college planning. Before you know it, their student is a Junior or Senior in high school, and they are desperately trying to plan for college. I guarantee this is a great way to feel extremely stressed out by this process. Parents often ask me when the best time to start college planning is, and I tell them, "When your child is born." Most parents procrastinate, so start planning now and you won't get caught unprepared.

In the next chapter, we'll be talking about some of the common myths of college planning. By the time you're done, you will hopefully have some new insights about this process. And like I said, try to keep an open mind, and I guarantee that you will see there are opportunities out there for everyone.

CHAPTER 3

You've Been Lied to ... Top Ten College Planning Myths

I remember my first day of college, the rush and excitement of seeing so many unfamiliar faces, wandering the halls exploring the enormous Michigan State campus, and trying to figure out which buildings my classes were in. My dorm was typical, small and very basic, with two bedrooms and a bathroom in between (which the four of us often fought over). My roommate was a friend of mine from high school.

Like a lot of middle income families, my parents had blindly assumed they made too much to qualify for financial aid. As a result, my first year of college, I worked fifteen to twenty hours a week in addition to a full load of classes. I did landscaping work, and also worked in food services on campus, but the job was so terrible I only lasted a few weeks.

I began to notice right away that not all students had the same insane schedule as me. My roommate, for instance, had his college paid for. Unlike mine, his parents had his tuition covered so he didn't have to work. He'd be out at the bars, hanging out with friends on the weekends, and I'd be working. While I was enormously proud of being able to pay for my own tuition, I definitely felt like I got cheated out of some of the college experiences.

My roommate was from a middle class family, the same as mine. I wondered, *how is this possible?* How were his parents able to afford his tuition? Then one day he mentioned he got financial aid.

Financial aid!

This piqued my interest. I hadn't even considered financial aid, nor did I even fully understand it, obviously, because I had assumed we made too much money. Suddenly, I wondered if we had known there was financial aid available would that have changed things? *What else did we get wrong?* Clearly there was a lot more to this college planning thing than I had realized...

Planning for college is more than just selecting an institution to attend, getting admitted, and showing up for classes. Most students planning on continuing their education beyond high school approach the educational experience with blinders on, and many parents that attended college in the past, believe that the college planning process is no different than what they went through school twenty or more years ago ... apply to colleges, get admitted, pack your bags, and off you go!

As a result, a lot of parents are operating under false information when they embark on putting their children through college. Also, how individuals pay for the cost of a college education has changed drastically over the last twenty or thirty years. There are many myths floating around that most parents and students believe is the absolute truth—such as, who gets financial aid (it's not always who you think), how to apply for scholarships, whether private colleges are really better, and so on. As we all know, hindsight is 20/20, and I definitely wish my parents and I had access to this information when I was applying to colleges. So, in this chapter, we will outline the top ten myths and put them to rest.

Here are the top ten myths (and realities) of paying for college:

Myth #1: Private Colleges Are Too Expensive for the Average Family

While it is true that private colleges do show a higher cost of attending than most public supported universities, they are not automatically more expensive than state universities.

Normally, private colleges receive very little money from the state that they are located in. Therefore, without state financial support, they must show a higher sticker cost than state-supported universities on paper. But they are still a business, and like all businesses, they have competitors. In order to compete (cost-wise) with state-supported universities, private college must adjust their total cost of attending to avoid losing potential students to other lower priced colleges. The little known secret is that in order for the private universities to stay competitive with state universities, they will usually offset these higher costs by providing institutional financial aid to students in the form of need- and merit-based scholarships and grants.

With the added benefits of institutional financial aid, many private colleges wind up being less expensive than state-supported colleges. Which means that private colleges being exclusive to elites is a myth.

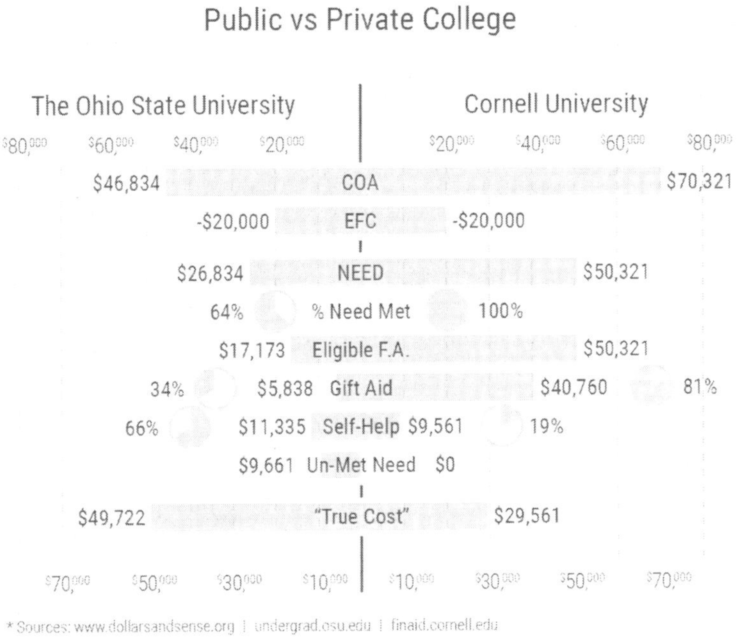

Myth #2: Saving Money to Help Pay for College Will Reduce My Financial Aid Eligibility

The first thing families need to understand is that financial aid from the Federal and State governments is intended to help the neediest students to attend college. It is true financial aid is given out mostly based on the financial need of the family. However, the majority of financial aid given out through the Federal government is in the form of student and parent loans. When completing the Free Application for Student Aid (FAFSA), the formula calculates the amount of savings that will be used to help pay for college expenses as only 5.65 percent for the parents and 20 percent for the student. Also, the parent receives what is called an asset protection allowance to help offset some of the savings.

With this being the case, the amount of savings that are in the parent's name will be reduced by a certain dollar amount. For example, if the parents had an asset protection allowance of $7,000 and saved $20,000 to help pay for their student's college education, the Federal formula will only require $735 (the first year) to be used to help pay for the student's college costs.

This is very important to remember: having assets saved to help pay for the cost of a college education is not the biggest factor when it comes to receiving financial aid. The largest factor that will affect financial aid eligibility is **income**, not assets. If the family does elect to save for the cost of a college education, it is better to save money in the parent's name instead of the student's name. The reason for this is that assets in the parent's name are only assessed at 5.65 percent, while assets saved in the student's name will be assessed at a 20 percent level. Another disadvantage in saving money in the student's name is that, unlike the parents, the student won't receive an asset protection allowance.

Myth #3: The Myth of the Unclaimed Scholarship Funds

I get asked this question a lot by clients: Are there millions of scholarship dollars going unclaimed each year?

This myth has been circulating in our school systems for decades. There are even college planning books that come out every year touting this myth, the myth that there are millions of dollars of college scholarships going unclaimed each year ... but this is totally false.

Nonprofit and for-profit organizations distribute millions of dollars in scholarship funds each year, based on certain criteria. These funds are distributed to needy and/or talented students.

However, the funds are only given out if the donor's investment portfolio is adequate to allocate the funds. There are scholarships given out by Rotary Clubs, churches, and Men's/Women's Groups as well. Also, these funds are given out on a very competitive standpoint, and the average high school student who shows no need or talent (academically, athletically, etc.) will not qualify for most of these scholarships. Most of the unclaimed scholarships come from employee benefit programs under IRS regulation Section 127 Educational Assistance programs, which is mostly available to employees of corporations or small business owners.

So, if most of these nonprofit and for-profit organizations are giving out all the money they can, where are all the millions of dollars in college scholarship funds going unclaimed?

Nowhere, because they don't exist.

Myth #4: Scholarships and Grants Will Reduce My Expected Family Contribution (EFC)

Let's say you have just completed the Free Application for Federal Student Aid (FAFSA), and your expected family contribution is $15,000. The college your son or daughter has elected to attend has an annual cost of $30,000 a year, therefore, their financial need is $15,000. Fortunately, your child is a great student, and they were also honored to receive a $1,000 scholarship from the local Rotary club.

You assume, since the student will receive a $1,000 scholarship from the Rotary club, your expected family contribution would be reduced to $14,000, not $15,000. However, it doesn't work this way. Most colleges will count the scholarship from the Rotary Club as an outside resource and will adjust the student's financial aid offer accordingly.

For example, let's assume the original financial aid offer was as follows:

- **$3,500 subsidized Federal loan**
- **$2,000 in unsubsidized Federal loan**

- **$2,000 in need-based scholarship**
- **$7,500 in Parents PLUS loan**

Since the student received a $1,000 scholarship from the Rotary Club, the college reduced the $2,000 scholarship that the college first offered down to $1,000. Thus, leaving the parents (you) to pay for the full $15,000 Expected Family Contribution.

The reason this occurs is that most colleges count scholarships not given directly by the college as part of a student's financial assets and offer aid accordingly, rather than allocating those funds from the Families Expected Contribution (EFC).

Need Based Formula

Based on the Needs Analysis Formula

COA: Cost of Attendance	$25,000
EFC: Expected Family Contribution	-$15,000
"Financial Need"	$10,000

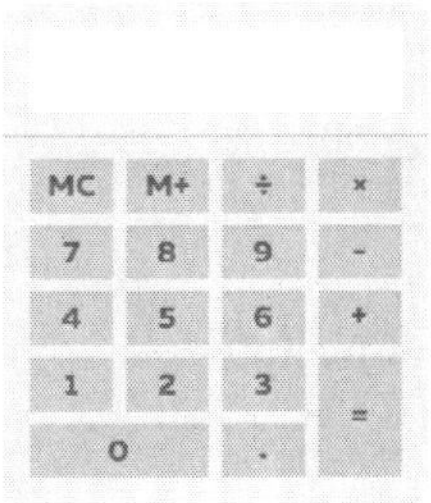

Myth #5: Scholarships and Grants Are Always Tax-Free

Colleges and universities define scholarships and grants as funds for the benefit of the student based on the need of the student, or on his or her merit. On the other hand, the IRS defines scholarships and grants as **qualified**, **non-qualified**, **restrictive,** and **nonrestrictive**.

The IRS does not care whether the scholarship or grant was given to the student based on need or merit; however, the IRS is concerned as to how the scholarship or grant is to be used. If the scholarship or grant is used to pay for qualified educational expenses, the scholarship or grant is tax-free to the student. If the funds are being used to pay for non-qualified expenses, the scholarship or grant is taxable to the student.

Myth #6: Middle and High-Income Families Are out of Luck and Won't Qualify for Free Financial Aid Dollars from the Federal Government

Many middle and high-income families are under the assumption that they won't qualify for free money from the Federal and State governments. However, this is not totally true. The largest program that provides free money from the Federal government is the Pell grant program. In a few unique situations, high and middle-income earning families could qualify for a Pell grant. Most parents think the Pell grant is based on the financial need of the household. In reality, the Pell grant has nothing to do with a family's financial need. Pell grant money is given out based on the family's expected contribution, better known as your EFC.

The most prominent driving factor in calculating your EFC is your adjusted gross income. If you make a substantial amount of money but have a significant amount of business or other losses, it could drop your adjusted gross income to a level that would cause your EFC to fall into the guidelines of qualifying for the Pell grant. Over the course of my career, I have seen families that made six-figure salaries, but due to their business or other losses causing their adjusted gross income to be small, still qualified them for the Pell grant.

Myth #7: If a Student Borrows from the Federal Student Loan Program, They Must Pay All of the Principle and Interest on the Loan until It Is Paid in full

According to the College Board, there is approximately $1.5 trillion in student loan debt that has been amassed over the last several years. In the past, most families were able to pay for a college education with little or no debt at all. However, borrowing for college is now the norm.

In the past, all students had college debt repayment schedules set at a ten-year payback. However, today, there are several options in which the student can pay back their student loans. There are income-driven payback programs which are tied to the borrower's discretionary income. Under one plan, if a student works for a public service entity, their remaining loan balance after ten years of payments could be forgiven even though they have a balance remaining. If the student works in the private sector, they can have their loan balance forgiven after twenty or twenty-five years.

Myth #8: I Expect to Receive a Lot of Scholarships outside the College System, Therefore I Don't Need to Complete the Financial Aid Applications

If you're expected to receive a lot of scholarships from outside resources, you are normally classified as a high academic or highly recruitable student. Therefore, you could qualify for merit-based scholarships from the college that you will be attending. However, normally colleges will not distribute nor offer scholarships to the student, whether or not based off of need or merit, *until* the financial aid applications are completed. Therefore, if you do not complete the financial aid applications, you could be leaving a lot of free money on the table.

Myth #9: My Parents Make Too Much Money to Qualify for Any Aid

It is true, wealthier families normally will not qualify for need-based scholarships or grants. However, there are several different types of financial strategies available. There are dozens of options available that will lower the cost of college. It is always wise to complete the FAFSA in order to see what you may qualify for based on the cost of the college you will be attending. Your family may have certain circumstances that could increase the chances of getting some aid. Certain circumstances could include the number of students in the household that will be attending college at the same time, the household size, medical circumstances, and the age of the oldest parent, just to name a few.

Financial Aid: Who Is Eligible?

Myth vs Reality

- Income too high
- Grades too low
- Own a home
- Aid is only for special groups
- School people can help
- It's an easy process

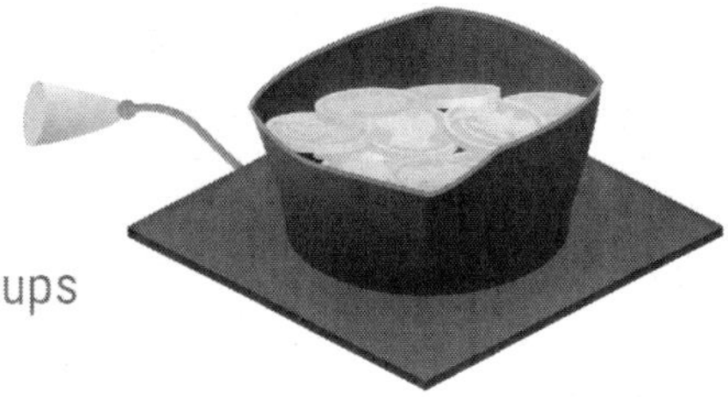

Myth #10: We Don't Have to Worry about Applying for Financial Aid... My Kid Isn't Even a Senior in High School Yet

This is the biggest mistake of all! Postponing the inevitable is the biggest pitfall for parents. What if you were age sixty-five and you turned to your wife and said, "I guess it's time for us to start saving for retirement!" This is the same type of mistake families make when it comes to planning for how to pay for college expenses. Trying to make financial decisions at the very last minute will cause many financial mistakes to be made. Learning about whether or not you will qualify for financial aid and how to pay for college expenses should start when your children are very young, or at least no later than the student's Freshman year in high school.

Now that we've addressed some of the most common myths about college planning—and hopefully dispelled them—it's time for another "truth bomb." In the next chapter, we'll be exploring the truth about college planning and your retirement.

CHAPTER 4

The Truth About College and Retirement: What You Don't Know Now Could Cost You Thousands of Dollars Later

The other day some new clients came into my office for a college planning assessment. After shaking hands and introducing themselves, the married couple sat down across from my desk. They were well-dressed and composed, but I couldn't help but notice the worried expressions on their faces.

I asked them a few basic questions at first, trying to assess where they were at in the planning process, like, "what colleges are you looking at?" and "how old are your kids?" After a few minutes of this, the husband interrupted me.

He said, "Honestly, I've been looking at the numbers ... and I don't believe I can pay for college and still have a retirement."

They are a hard working middle class family with savings, and they are struggling just to put one of their kids through college without risking their retirement. They aren't the only ones, either.

How do I pay for college and still retire? It's a question that's on many peoples' minds in America.

How Will You Pay For College?

Financial Aid
- Scholarship
- Grants
- Tuition Discounts
- Need-Based Financial Aid

Borrow
- College Loans
- Home Loan
- ~~Retirement~~

Assets
- Savings
- Investment

Income
- Current Paycheck
- Retirement Contributions

Gifts
- ??????

The truth is, it's a two-part problem.

Paying for the cost of a college education and saving for your own financial future at the same time can be difficult and sometimes it may seem impossible to do both. With the natural uncertainty of the stock market and college costs continuing to outpace the national inflation rate, many families, such as this one, are being forced to choose between saving for their personal financial future or paying for their student's college education.

I saw a headline the other day in a recent financial industry publication declaring: "Market's Woes Complicate Retirement Planning." In the article, the author made the statement that, "Some investors will take less from their nest eggs—or keep working."

As a college planner, I can say from firsthand experience, that this is true.

These headlines are not the exceptions to the rule but the norm in financial publications across the nation. If you've been paying attention at all to the media lately, the concepts of bear markets and taking less or working more during retirement has been forecasted throughout our society over the last thirty or forty years.

Planning for future income needs and knowing how to pay for college expenses has forced many families to choose one or the other, and as a result, many financial professionals try to separate the two altogether. They feel each are separate problems and should be dealt with individually.

This is a fundamental mistake, in my opinion. I believe paying for college and saving for future income needs are two problems rolled into one. Both are complicated and interdependent, and to think otherwise is being naive.

Let's look at the statistics around retirement and college debt in the modern age.

BILLIONS IN COLLEGE STUDENT LOAN DEBT IS HELD BY ADULTS FIFTY-PLUS

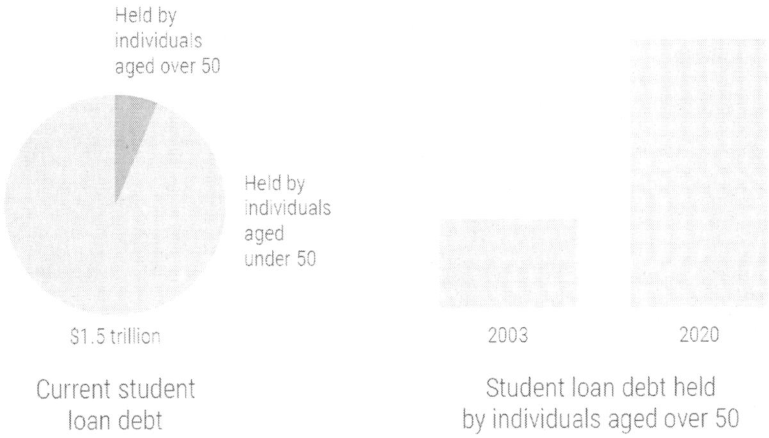

As of the present, there are over $1.5 trillion dollars of college student loan debt in America. However, what is not being reported, is that $247 billion dollars of college student loan debt is being held by individuals over the age of 50. Individuals over the age of 50 that have student loan debts have more than tripled since 2003 according to a recent report by the Urban Institution.

A recent survey by the Urban Institute found that 3.5 percent of Americans over the age of fifty hold student loans that they took out for their own education and 8 percent hold loans for their children or grandchildren. We all know that student loan debt is one type of debt that can't be dismissed in bankruptcy and according to the U.S. Government Accountability Office, the Federal government is withholding a portion of Social Security benefits from thousands of older Americans that are in default on their own college loans.

That means more adults than ever are approaching retirement saddled with student loan debt from children, or even grandchildren, they've put through college.

According to the Urban Institute survey, 55 percent of adults over the age of fifty are struggling with money issues as compared to only 33 percent of younger borrowers. The survey also reported African American adults over the age of fifty are three times more likely to have money issues than their white counterparts, mainly due to their own student loan debts.

This chart is from the Urban Institution, showing that African Americans hold more personal student loans than their white or Hispanic peers. It also shows individuals making less than $20,000 a year hold more personal student loan debt than individuals making $100,000 a year plus.

However, individuals making over $100,000 a year have approximately 13 percent of student loan debt taken out for their children or grandkids.

Education Debt Among Americans Aged 50 and Older

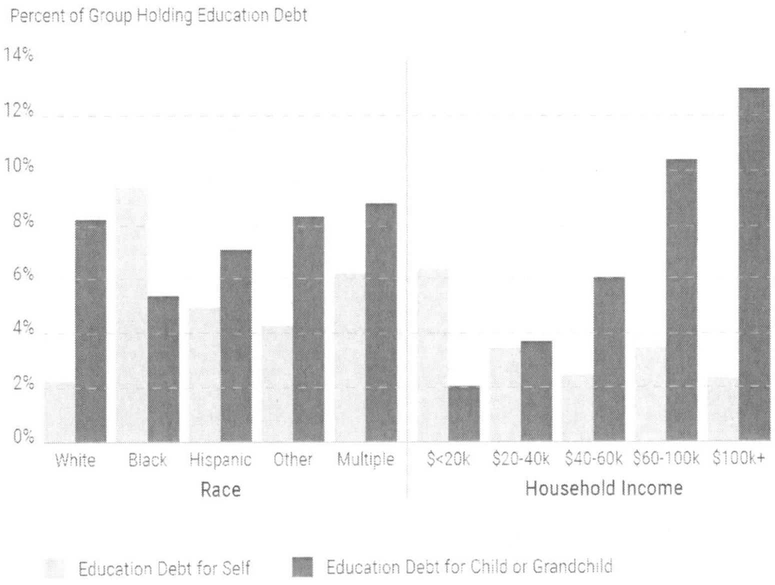

Source: Urban Institute analysis of SHED Data from 2013 to 2016.
Note: Holding debt for a child or grandchild is reported all respondents, regardless of if they report having children.

In 2015, the United States Department of Education collected $171 million of the $4.5 billion of student loan debt that is in default from individuals that are receiving Social Security benefits.

Also, according to the Department of Education, 43 percent of adults over the age of fifty have held student loan debt for twenty years or more and three-quarters of older borrowers have taken loans only for their own education.

Some of the $247 billion in student loan debt held by individuals over the age of fifty have borrowed to help pay for college expenses by using credit cards to pay for their children or grandchildren's college education.

Also, according to the Department of Education, many older adults who have borrowed to help pay for their children or grandchildren are more than likely current on their debt payment.

However, 31 percent of older borrowers that borrowed for their own education are behind or in default on their student loans.

This chart shows the financial security among Americans age fifty and older with educational debt.

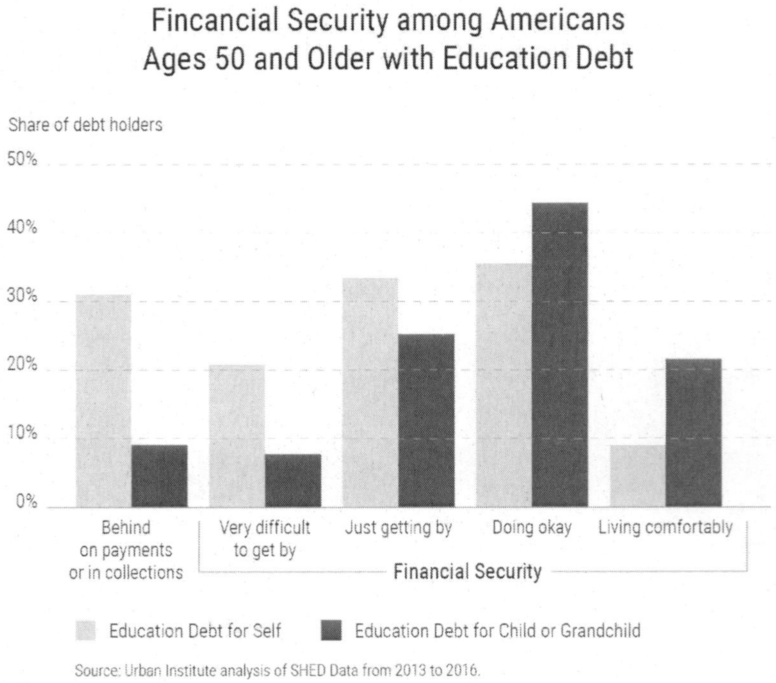

Another report by the Consumer Financial Protection Bureau found individuals "60 and older is the fastest growing age segment with student debt, and nearly 40 percent of borrowers 65 and older are in default. Many individuals in this age group borrow the money in their own name, or they are cosigning for their children or grandchildren."

No matter who finds themselves with student loan debt, somewhere down the road it will affect your future income needs as well as future borrowing needs, such as taking out or paying down a mortgage, car loans, medical bills, and other necessary debt obligations.

So you see, lack of proper college planning can greatly affect your ability to retire comfortably in today's world. To compound the problems retiring adults are facing is the fact that traditional pensions have almost entirely disappeared, 401Ks and IRAs are less than ideal vehicles for retirement savings (I will get into this more in depth later in the book), and Social Security is likely going to change (if not completely disappear) in the next few decades.

If you're in despair right now, don't be. I've been able to help more than a thousand families through college and retirement planning, and just like I told the couple whom I mentioned earlier who were at their wit's end sitting in my office that day, "You can do both."

Complex problems, like retirement and college, require sophisticated solutions. And there is always a solution. It just might not be the obvious one.

Savers Vs. Non-Savers

Most people assume the solution is to simply "save more money" for college—my answer is yes, and no.

Some families are savers, and others aren't. Savings isn't a panacea, because those families that have saved up money, likely still need help. Or, as I like to ask my clients—*why use your own money if you don't have to?*

To those families that don't have money saved, I say—*let's find money!*

In my experience, everyone can be helped. No matter how much savings they're starting out with. For most families, it's all about preemptive planning, having the right strategy, researching the best schools, and finding money—not saving money.

In fact, the biggest problem for most parents isn't lack of resources, it's procrastination.

Most families put off planning for college until the student's Senior year in high school and this is where the problem really begins. You can't, or it is very difficult—if not impossible—to solve a $90,000 to a $250,000 problem in a few months, let alone a few years without professional help.

No one should ever say, "It's too late, we can't plan," but if you're just starting to prepare yourself financially for college and your child is already a Freshman in high school, you're going to have a lot harder time than if you had started earlier.

Keep in mind, once you have a plan in place, you still have to plan—for unforeseen obstacles, for changes in your life or health, for sudden shifts in the economy, etc. In a way, the planning never ends—if you're sixty-five years old, you're still actively planning for retirement. So, I'd like you to get used to planning. Plan now, plan early, and plan for every possible scenario.

The second thing you need to do is arm yourself with as much knowledge as possible.

You Need to Become More Knowledgeable

Normally, most parents only hear one side of the story when it comes to paying for college expenses. They're taking advice from well-meaning friends and family, or maybe digging around on the internet to find out more information. The sad part of this scenario is the story they are likely hearing is causing them to pay more for a college education than they need to, and their retirement plans are suffering as a result.

Parents of college-bound students need to become more knowledgeable about the various options available to them when it comes to their own future income needs and paying for college. And a large part of that is finding the right professional to work with.

Today we have more students and parents borrowing for college than any time in our history. This borrowing has a drastic impact on the future financial lifestyle of the student and has an even more devastating impact on the parents' future retirement goals. In other words, the more the parents borrow, the less money they have available to save for their own future financial needs.

If you are working with a financial professional, they should be providing guidance to you for living off your present income and giving you ideas on how to pay for college expenses *without* depending on financial aid, while saving for retirement at the same time.

If they aren't doing this, then you need to seek out a better source of guidance than you currently have. The mistakes you are making today could potentially cost you thousands in the long run.

This chapter is both a wakeup call and also a silver lining for parents who might be worried about how they're going to afford it all. There's no need to worry, with the right information and enough of a head start, you can both retire comfortably and afford to put your kids through college.

Once again, I believe paying for college and saving for your future income needs are two problems rolled into one. Both are complicated and to think you can do it without a solid plan, or only hearing one side of the story, is naive. So, wrap your head around the idea of planning now, educate yourself on your options, and don't delay.

As you'll see in the next chapter, you're going to need as much information as possible, because parents aren't the only ones doing the scamming.

CHAPTER 5

Don't Fall for Student Loan and Scholarship Scams

It was the summer of 1984, and I was ten years old. We were on a family vacation in New York City, visiting my aunt and uncle on Long Island. We made a day trip to the city to walk around and check out the popular tourist destinations such as Columbus Circle and the Met. As we were walking past some large department stores uptown, I got distracted by something I saw in one of the windows, I looked away for just a moment—and suddenly I was alone, surrounded by a sea of complete strangers going about their business.

I've never felt so scared in my life. I ran around the block, dodging what seemed like thousands of people on the crowded sidewalk, crying out, "Mom! Dad!"

No answer.

I started begging people, going up to total strangers, pleading with them to please help me find my parents. Being alone, in this overwhelming, strange, and unfamiliar place was absolutely terrifying. Finally, after what seemed like an eternity, a nicely dressed man and woman on their way to work noticed me standing there with tears in my eyes.

They offered to call the police and get me reunited with my family. Then they stood there with me, waiting for the cops to arrive. Fifteen minutes later, I heard a familiar voice calling my name. It was my dad, he had spotted me and was standing on the corner shouting my name. I ran over to him, and immediately felt this heavy weight lift off of me.

It turned out my family thought I was with them as they went into a bookstore, and that's why it took them a few minutes to realize I was missing. How nice of that couple to stop and help a distressed young boy, when hundreds of others didn't even give me the time of day.

Anything could have happened to me that day. I was very lucky and blessed to have help when I needed it the most. When I think back on this memory, all I can remember is that couple's kindness, and the compassion of those good hearted people.

To me, there aren't enough of these helpful good Samaritans in the world. It seems there's a lot more of the other kind of people, who would just as likely leave you stranded and alone. Or worse.

We're aware of parents trying to scam the system, but what about people who scam *parents*?

Unfortunately, it does exist.

In recent years, the skyrocketing cost of college has forced many families to look for alternative ways of paying for the cost of a college education. Students, as well as their parents, are borrowing more money to help pay for college expenses than ever before. This leaves parents in a vulnerable position, which creates a tempting invitation for scammers.

Living Pay Check to Pay Check?

65% of American families rely on their next pay check to meet their monthly living expenses

Only 4% of American families have **saved** $5,000 or more at the time their child enters college

A recent report from the Federal Department of Education said, "The proportion of students borrowing to pursue college degrees was up in 2015-16 compared to eight years prior, according to Federal data. The average amount borrowed increased by nearly $6,000 over the same period. Of students who completed their degree in the 2007-08 academic year, 65.6 percent took out student loans, borrowing $24,700 on average. Eight years later, 67.4 percent of students took out loans, borrowing an average of $30,500."

With borrowing at an all-time high, families are driven to search for scholarships to help pay for the cost of a college education and keep borrowing down to a minimum. However, searching for scholarships could be a dangerous endeavor. There are many predatory companies that are offering scholarship funds that could be detrimental to the student as well as their parents.

Many of these scholarship search scams are promising scholarship funds to students once they have completed a lengthy and personal survey. Once registered, the student may receive spam emails that could contain misleading U.S. Department of Education logos emblazoned across websites asking for an upfront fee to apply.

The latest data from the Federal Trade Commission's report said, "It received 725 consumer reports of problems related to scholarships and educational grants in 2018. This data is based only on consumer reports of issues, and therefore, do not reflect the actual number of fraudulent incidents."

Yikes.

The Better Business Bureau has also issued a warning that there could be an increase in scholarship and student loan scam programs for the year 2019 and beyond. Families that are looking for scholarship opportunities should be very cautious of suspicious websites and leery of official sounding emails notifying a student that they have won scholarship dollars.

John Breyault, Vice President of Public Policy of the Federal Trade Commission, said, "The FTC has identified hundreds of complaints every year about these scholarship or educational grant scams. But what's just as interesting is how many students are complaining to them about fraud related to the student loan industry. So, it's unclear whether those student loan complaints are encompassing offerings that are scam scholarships as well, and those numbers are in the thousands."

Let's look at the different types of fraud and schemes you should watch out for.

Debt Relief

Everyone wants to pay down debt as quickly as possible. Scammers know this and can use it to lure parents and students into debt consolidation and debt relief scams.

There are more than 42 million Americans that owe a total of $1.5 trillion in college loan debt. According to the Federal Trade Commission, **"Scammers are targeting borrowers with student loan debt relief schemes that can actually make things worse."**

In a new case announced on July 11th, 2019, by the Federal Trade Commission publicized that, "Today, the FTC alleges the operators of Mission Hills Federal and Federal Direct Group bilked borrowers out of more than $23 million. These companies lured people with false promises to pay down student loans and lower monthly payments. The companies also lied about taking over the servicing of the loans, which tricked people into submitting loan payments directly to them. In fact, the defendants diverted borrower payments to themselves."

Identity Theft

According to the FTC's report, "Federal student loan identity theft reports in 2018 were up 119 percent over the previous year, and consumer reports of student loan problems with banks and lenders in 2018 numbered 29,346.

Katherine Hutt, the spokeswoman for the Council of Better Business Bureaus, Inc, said, "Students are prime targets for scholarship and student loan scams. A combination of inexperience, vulnerability, and desperation as college costs increase and states cut funding for public institutions create a perfect storm.

Students represented 9.4 percent of fraud reports submitted to the BBB Scam Tracker in 2018, and about 24 percent of students reported a loss when exposed to a scam, compared with only about 28 percent of non-students."

The two biggest red flags of a scholarship scam are when students are notified they have won scholarship funds that they have never applied for and they want the student to pay a fee to be eligible to receive the funds.

HOW TO AVOID A SCHOLARSHIP OR STUDENT LOAN SCAM:

Here are a few things that students, as well as parents, should know to avoid falling for a scholarship and loan scam.

- Never provide your Social Security number or bank account information to a scholarship or loan program before making sure it's a viable and reputable program
- Never pay an upfront application fee and never provide credit card information
- Ask for a list of past award winners, and if possible, contacts previous winners
- Ask the scholarship and loan program to communicate with you in writing. If the program will not communicate with you by written communication, it normally could be a red flag and the resource could be dealing in fraudulent activities

REPUTABLE SCHOLARSHIP SEARCH WEBSITES AND RESOURCES:

The best resource for finding and applying for scholarships is in your local community. The best source to check on these resources is from your high school guidance counselor.

Here are a few reputable and free scholarship websites and resources.

- **Scholarships.com:** tracks $19 billion in scholarships.
- **Fastweb.com:** has 1.5 million scholarships in its database.
- **Chegg.com:** has 25,000 scholarships resources.
- **Cappex.com:** has $11 billion in scholarships.
- **JLV College Counseling:** offers information on various scholarships every Saturday.
- **The College Board:** has information on colleges and more than $6 billion in scholarships.
- **Niche.com:** this site pairs students with the scholarships that match their qualifications.
- **Community foundation website:** should list local scholarship availabilities.
- **College websites that you are interested in attending:** scholarships and amounts will vary from college to college.

Now that you know what to look for when it comes to scholarship and loan scams, let's look at a few ideas that families can use to increase the potential of the student to receive scholarship funds.

- **GPA** - Keep the student's GPA above 3.0 (taking advanced courses when available) all the way through high school.
- **Get Involved** - Student should get involved in extracurricular activities in and out of the high school environment.

- **Get Organized** - Learning organizational skills will make studying and learning much easier.
- **Start Looking Early** - Students should start looking at potential colleges as early as the Sophomore year in high school. Things to consider are academic programs, social, atmosphere, location, student body, etc. In other words, select colleges that are a right fit for the student.
- **ACT/SAT** - Scoring high on either of these two tests are essential when it comes to getting admitted to the student's selected college, as well as positioning the student for scholarships.

One last word of advice, never apply for scholarships or student loans with the following promise in it:

"The scholarship or loan is guaranteed—or your money back."

And finally, if it just seems too good to be true, it probably is. Always use your gut instinct, as well as your common sense when evaluating what looks like an easy opportunity.

As you can see, this book has a theme to it: shortcuts and scams never pay in the end. That being said, there are still some very clever ways to make the system work better for you, without having to resort to dangerous tactics. One of them, as you'll see in the next chapter, is having the IRS help pay for college.

CHAPTER 6

How the IRS Can Help Pay for College

Several years ago, I was introduced to a woman named Jennifer who later became a college planning client of mine. During our first meeting, we discovered we were neighbors, actually; she was living in the same neighborhood as me. Jennifer had two kids entering college soon, they were a middle income family, making over six figures a year.

Like many other parents, Jennifer knew she would have to rely mostly on financial aid to help pay for most of her son and daughter's college tuition. But the rest of the college day-to-day expenses would be on her. Jennifer really wanted her kids to focus 100 percent on their studies, she didn't want them trying to juggle a full- or part-time job while they were enrolled.

As we reviewed some of the expected non-tuition costs, such as expensive textbooks, supplies, transportation, on-campus meals, and lab fees, Jennifer's demeanor changed. She confessed she wasn't sure how she would be able to afford it all—without dipping into her retirement savings, or severely limiting her lifestyle.

"I wish there was some way to offset some of the other college costs," she said.

"There is," I told her.

"What if we used the IRS to help pay for your kids' college?"

Her eyebrows lifted in surprise. "The *IRS*?"

Through talking with her, Jennifer revealed to me that she had a small homebased business. Every year during the holidays, she crafted and sold handmade gift baskets with jellies, chocolates, and cookies online. It was "more of a hobby" as she described it, but I knew there was potential here for extra cash, and tax savings.

Fortunately, Jennifer was open to the idea.

Let the IRS Help Pay for Your Child's College Education

- **American Opportunity Tax Credit**
  $2,500 maximum
- **Lifetime Learning Credit**
  $2,000 maximum
- **Hope Scholarship**
- The deduction may be the same as scholarship
- Higher tax bracket, means greater the benefit
- IRS rules allow you to keep more money

* Note: This is for informational purposes only and should not be construed as tax advice. Please consult your tax advisor.
* Source: www.irs.gov

I explained to her that in reality, the Federal Financial Aid system is directly affiliated with the Internal Revenue Service. And her home-based business was the key to recovering some of those non-tuition college costs.

We laid out a strategy for Jennifer to scale her home-based business, so she was able to write off her expenses, and offset some of the taxes she'd be paying while she was putting her daughter and son through college. This way her own retirement savings and the comfort of her current lifestyle wouldn't be impacted.

Meanwhile, I researched schools and found programs that worked well for her son and daughter and helped secure those for them. Fortunately, both students met the criteria for significant scholarship awards, and I guided them toward those schools.

Jennifer's daughter got accepted to the University of Dayton, a private school in Ohio. Her son went to Western Michigan, a state funded school. As expected, both received some financial aid, especially from the University of Dayton, her daughter got $68,000 in grants, and her son received $12,000 over four years. These were scholarship grants, so it was basically free money from the schools.

In addition to the tax savings we were able to get, Jennifer comfortably helped her children get through all four years of college without worrying about her own financial security.

If you're anything like Jennifer, you probably didn't realize that your home-based business could be a huge asset when planning for college. Most college-bound parents don't think of the IRS as a benevolent ally in this process. In reality, if you are strategic about your tax planning, and how you complete your income tax returns, you could create what we call a Tax Scholarship, which could be more valuable than financial aid or scholarships.

In this chapter, we'll be exploring strategies for creating your own Tax Scholarship, no matter what tax bracket your family is in.

A Brief History of Two Types of Taxpayers

The financial aid formula runs off of parents' and students' income tax returns, and contrary to popular belief, income is the largest factor when it comes to qualifying for financial aid, not assets. As a result, many middle- and high-income taxpayers will not qualify for as much need-based financial aid at state-supported colleges and universities, as parents with less income. This is where a strategic tax plan and a home-based business can make a huge difference in your ability to pay for college.

The first thing you need to understand is there are **two** types of taxpayers:

- **W-2 wage earners and;**
- **Self-employed or business owner**

No one likes paying taxes. However, taxes must be paid in order to provide necessary services to the general society, such as defense, roads, and other items that benefit the majority of the nation's citizenry. Our tax system was not established to be used as a social welfare system. However, according to the Tax Foundation and other tax think tanks, most of our tax dollars are used to provide social benefits (Social Security, Medicare, Medicaid, Welfare, college financial aid, etc.). Many individuals feel that these social benefits are necessary for our society today. Regardless of your position, it is my belief that individuals should only pay their **fair share** and no more.

Today it is almost impossible to raise a family and provide a college education to children without both parents working. Of course, the more you make, the more taxes you will pay to the Federal and State Taxing Authorities.

According to the Tax Foundation, "Individuals that have earned income and paid taxes, will pay more in taxes than they pay for food, clothing, and shelter combined."

There are very few things a W-2 wage earner can do to reduce their taxes (other than adjustments to income and itemized deductions)—or control the amount of taxes they will pay. However, if you have a home-based business or are a self-employed businessperson, there are thousands of ideas that can help reduce your taxes that can be used to help you pay for college, retirement, or simply reduce debt.

A home-based business allows you to not only control how you pay taxes, but also gives you the ability to reduce the taxation on the income you earn working your small business, and depending on how you structure your business, you can also potentially reduce the tax on your W-2 wages as well.

Before I get into telling you how to start a home-based business, I want to emphasize: Do not start a business just to get the tax write-offs. Remember, this is not a book on how to illegally scam the college system; we want completely ethical solutions here. The intent of starting a business should only be to earn additional income to help pay for college, invest in your retirement, and to reduce debt.

Always remember, the IRS does not tolerate scams and will shut you down if they think your business is a fake.

Real Home-Based Business vs. Fake Home-Based Business

According to Diane Kennedy (strategic tax planner and CPA: www.taxloopholes.com), a real home-based business will be one that acts like a business. It often operates through a business structure, keeps separate books and records, has separate bank accounts, prepares financial statements at least once a year and above all, operates with the expectation of making a profit.

However, this does not mean your business absolutely must make a profit. In fact, your business could lose money for years. Many legitimate businesses do.

A real business is usually semi-formal. It may be incorporated or otherwise formally organized, (DBA "doing business as") and have established systems in place to manage how services are provided, and how you get paid (i.e., work orders and invoices). There will be administrative aspects of a real business, such as recordkeeping and bookkeeping, and there are strict financial controls on where the money is deposited and how it is withdrawn. Real businesses also prepare proper financial statements.

A fake home based business, on the other hand, is a business that only exists for one reason: to make a loss!

It does not sell or do anything, it exists solely as a method to move regular living expenses into the pre-tax dollar column. Diane Kennedy used this example, "Putting a filing cabinet into a room and claiming the home office deduction for that entire room."

A fake business may be something you do to make a little extra money, but it does not necessarily exist to make a profit. Sewing baby clothes for your friends or acting as a dog trainer could easily be a business without a profit motive. In both cases, you are doing something that you enjoy and would be doing it anyway.

Also, a fake home-based business does not keep any special records, and probably doesn't have any special bookkeeping procedures in place. The money you make gets deposited into your personal account, and you spend your own money on supplies and things you need to carry out your fake business. You do not prepare financial statements, and simply declare the extra income on your tax return (at least I hope you do).

If you are thinking about starting a home-based business just for the tax benefits, expect audits, fines, penalties, and more.

It's okay to make a loss if you can show that you are **trying** to earn additional income or trying to establish a business that can turn into a full-time occupation.

What are the IRS Guidelines?

The IRS has outlined nine requirements that everyone must follow in order to have a legitimate business. Keep in mind, this does not mean you have to meet all nine at the same time. The most essential requirements are only the first two. As long as you follow these steps, you have a legitimate business and are entitled to all of the tax savings and deductions that are available for all businesses.

The most critical requirement of the nine steps is:

1. Your business must be organized and operated with the intention of making a profit.

The key word in this statement is intention. Making a profit is not an IRS requirement. The IRS knows many new businesses lose money for the first three to five years, and sometimes for much longer periods of time.

The next most important factor in proving you have a valid business is:

2. You carry on your activities in a businesslike manner.

This means keeping records that are in line with what is called generally accepted accounting principles, or GAAP. Also, you need to keep the business finances (income, expenses, etc.) separate from your personal finances.

Important Note: Do not operate your business through your personal checking account and make sure you keep all business-related receipts separate from your personal receipts. Your business records should have things like copies of all invoices, records of your sales, receipts for all of the merchandise and inventory purchases you have made over the year, as well as receipts for other things, like shipping supplies, postage, and so on.

This is not as complicated as it sounds and only takes a few minutes a day to get organized. Just make sure you document your business expenses fully.

The other seven steps are:

3. You depend on income from the activity for your livelihood.

For example, your primary objective is to earn as much income as possible, and the money that you earn is used to meet your living expenses. Alternatively, you may have cut back your regular employment hours to part-time, or even leave your job altogether and rely solely on your business income. The income from your business does not have to be your primary source of earnings, though.

4. Your losses are due to circumstances beyond your control (or are normal in the startup phase of your type of business).

It is okay for you to make a loss, as long as you document why, i.e., non-paying customers or fraud, cost of materials or overhead increased unexpectedly, etc. and you can show that those types of losses are typical for your type of business, especially in the beginning.

It is also helpful to learn what others in your business or similar business have experienced in terms of losses of profits.

5. You change your methods of operation in an attempt to improve profitability.

For example, if you provide a service and are paid after the service is provided and a few of your customers do not pay you, you need to change the way you are getting paid. If you are consistently losing money and not making a profit, do something to change the non-profitability like purchasing business books, attending seminars or marketing courses, and so on. You can also talk to business consultants, your CPA, or other experts about ways to make your business more profitable.

6. You or your advisors have the knowledge needed to carry on the activity as a successful business.

If you are brand new in your business, it does not make any sense to take advice from someone who has never operated your kind of business (or any other type of business) before. Someone needs to demonstrate some knowledge of your business!

7. You were successful in making a profit in similar activities in the past.

This does not necessarily mean you have run a business before, but if you have tried other business opportunities, it is helpful to be able to show that you have made a profit in the past.

8. The activity makes a profit in some years (how much profit it makes is also considered).

Your business has made a profit in at least some of the years it has been operating, and those profits have been large enough to make it economical to continue the business. This is often a tough step to fill in the early years, but this step is not as crucial in the early years as it becomes later on.

9. You can expect to make a future profit from the business and from appreciation of any assets used in the activity.

This is where putting your business profits to work for you comes in handy, especially if you can show that you are using your profits to invest in real estate, hire more employees, purchase more equipment, provide employee benefits and so on.

Now, you are not always going to meet all nine of these steps, and that is okay. Again, it is the first two steps that are critical.

Four Steps to Starting Your Home-Based Business

Now that you have a good general understanding of what is required to start a home-based business, let's discuss the actual steps:

STEP ONE - What Kind of Business Do You Want to Start?

The first thing you need to do is decide what type of business you want to start. If you haven't already decided, it may seem overwhelming at this stage, as there are a variety of businesses that you can establish—everything from babysitting, to accounting, to website building. However, to get you started, here are a list of some ideas:

- Consulting (what do you do for a living, turn it into a small business);
- Teaching classes on how to do things;
- Getting into a multi-level marketing program;
- Writing a book on what you know well and sell it on eBay;
- Tutoring students that are having trouble with a subject matter;
- Starting a lawn care, gutter cleaning, snow removal service;
- Becoming a proofreader;
- Becoming a seminar coordinator;
- Developing websites for churches or other business;
- And the list can go on and on.

The key is to do something that you know and can do well. Once you know what you want to do as a business, the next thing is to set up the business structure.

STEP TWO - Decide What Type of Business Structure to Use

There are several business structures you can establish. You can operate your business as a sole-proprietor, partnership, or you can incorporate your business as an LLC, S, or C corporation. Each of these structures has their advantages and disadvantages. Most of you will start your business as a sole-proprietor. This is the least costly and easy to set up. Typically, all you have to do is set up a business checking account and have the account listed as DBA - example: John Doe DBA (doing business as) Consulting Services of Greater Louisville.

If you are confused about which structure to use, I would recommend checking out a book from the library on business structures called, *Lower Your Taxes Big Time*, by Sandy Botkin, CPA, Esq., a former IRS Attorney and Senior Tax Law Specialist. Also, another great resource may be your CPA or tax specialist.

Note: Check with your local Taxing Authority to make sure you do not have to have a license to operate your business.

STEP THREE - Develop a Business Plan

It is always a good idea to develop a business plan to help you stay focused and keep your business on track. The plan does not have to be complex or filled with difficult legal terms and verbiage that is hard to understand. Below is a list of the bare minimums that should be in your business plan:

- Name and location of your business;
- Contact Information;
- How the business is structured (sole-proprietor, partnerships, LLC, S, or C Corporation, etc.);
- Brief overview of what the business does;
- Overview of your target market;
- Projected revenue for the first, second, and third years;
- Do you plan on hiring employees? (family members, children, outside contractors, etc.);
- Projected cost of running your business for the first, second, and third years;
- List of professionals that you can contact to help grow your business;
- And any other items that you feel are important to you and your business.

Keep in mind, your business plan does not have to be a novel, the length of the plan could be no more than a few pages. Once your business plan is written, make sure to file the plan in your business filing system.

STEP FOUR - Run Your Business Like a Business

Once the first four steps have been completed, you can start operating your business like a business.

Here are a few suggestions:

- Design a logo;
- Build a website;
- Have business cards printed;
- Print flyers notifying locals of your business opening;
- Run ads (Facebook, local papers, bulletin boards, etc.).

These four steps are essential when operating your new business. If you will notice, all of the steps we just went over covers the first two requirements of proving to the IRS that you have a real legitimate business and you are doing the right things in order to make a profit. As I said before, this is a real business's primary intent.

Now that you know how to set up your business, let's look at some of the business deductions you can legally deduct against your business income and, depending on how you structure your business, against your W-2 wages:

- Entertainment Costs
- Business Travel Expenses
- Home Office (portion of rent or mortgage)
- Transportation
- Catering
- Bank Fees
- Commissions
- Uniforms
- Business Phone, Internet, etc.
- Legal Fees

- Research Materials
- Supplies
- Equipment
- Business Vehicle

Note: *Keep in mind, this deduction list is approved by the IRS and is general in nature. The intent of listing these deductions is not intended to give legal, accounting, or investment advice and before implementing any of the items covered you should talk to your tax specialist or CPA to make sure the deduction can be taken.*

Establishing an Office in Your Home

You can deduct business usage expenses of certain costs dealing with your home as long as the area is **exclusively** used for business purposes. Below are the tax laws that must be followed:

- The home office is the principal place of business;
- The home office is used to meet clients or customers in the normal course of doing Business; or
- The home office is used as a day-care business.

What Deductions Are Available for a Home Office?

There are three categories that you need to know when it comes to home office deductions:

1. Expenses that are directly related to the home office portion.

Example: Painting your office, repairs, or other maintenance functions performed that are directly related to the space are 100 percent tax deductible.

2. Expenses that don't benefit the home office directly or indirectly.

Example: Painting another room, plumbing repairs of a bathroom or lawn care if you do not meet customers or clients at your home office are not tax deductible.

3. Indirect expenses related to the home in general.

This relates to depreciation, home security systems, utilities, repairs, painting of the outside of the home, etc. These deductions can be taken based on the percentage of the home office in relation to the total square footage of the home.

Example: If the square footage of your home office is 5 percent of the total square footage of the home, you can deduct 5 percent of these costs as business deductions.

It is essential to make sure that the home office expenses will stand up to an IRS audit. Below are a few suggestions that will help audit-proof your deductions. All these items should be filed in your business filing system:

- Take a picture of your home office;
- Figure out the square footage of your office space;
- Display your address and phone number on your business cards and flyers;
- If you have customers come to your office, have them sign a logbook;
- Keep records of the time you spend in your home office.

United State Treasury Secretary, Paul O'Neill once said, "A fine is a tax for doing something wrong. A tax is a fine for doing something right."

You will never pay less income tax as long as you are a W-2 wage earner. You must change the way you think about taxes and get out of the W-2 wage earner's trap. As long as it is set up legally, morally, and ethically, a home-based business can create additional income and reduce your taxes and allow you to use the extra money to help pay for your children's college education.

I hope this chapter has broadened your horizons a little bit, introduced some new strategies, and given you some ideas for your own family's college planning.

CHAPTER 7

How to Get the First Two Years of College for Free

Free college! Doesn't that sound great?

But should college be free?

Think about it. Would you have appreciated a college education if it were free? Or would you have taken it for granted? To be honest, I know I would have.

My first few years of college at Michigan State, I used my own money. I had "skin in the game," so to speak and it only made me apply myself harder and appreciate my education even more. I didn't mind the late nights studying, getting up at the crack of dawn to mow lawns, or working extra hard, because I knew at the end of the day it was coming from my paycheck. There was no way I was letting all those summers I spent working through high school go to waste.

If I had been given "free college," I might not have studied as hard, I might have done a lot more partying, and I certainly wouldn't have been as proud when I graduated, because I hadn't earned my way through college myself.

No matter what the media says about free education in America, it's unrealistic to expect free education anytime soon, and even if we did, it wouldn't completely devalue what having a diploma means in our society today. At the end of the day, most Americans want to work hard and pay for things themselves, and unless it's seeing their tax dollars at work, they don't want freebies or handouts.

If you haven't guessed, I'm not an advocate of free college. I believe students should have a vested interest in their college education, and some "skin in the game." It makes them work harder. If Mom, Dad, and the government are paying for everything, and they're getting an education for "free," it's just too easy to blow it off.

That being said, college should be financially accessible to everyone. And a big part of that is getting a great school that will step up to the plate with a grant or scholarship money.

There are three aspects of financial aid: free money (grants and scholarships), work study programs, and interest free student loans. Of course, everyone wants as much free money as they can get. At the end of the day, how much free money you receive is all dependent upon your financial situation, and the colleges you choose. Every school is different, and some schools are more generous than others, based on their endowments.

The key to college planning is not just randomly picking schools but choosing them based on actual financial data. The ultimate goal is to create a list of the top five or six schools you'd like your child to attend and get award letters from each of them. Then, you compare the awards and figure out, not just which school is best, but also which school is going to give you the most financial aid.

Don't be fooled by "name brand" schools, just because they're a large state funded institution, or a prestigious Ivy League University, that doesn't necessarily mean they hand out a lot of grants and scholarships. Michigan State, for instance, has a very large endowment, but they are not very generous in offering grants and scholarships. In many cases, smaller private universities give out more percentage wise than public universities.

Meeting a Student's Financial Need

Choose your college wisely, because:

- Not all will meet 100% of need

Private colleges generally:

- Meet a higher percentage of need
- Award a higher percentage of gift aid

Many Students can attend a private college for the **same** cost as a public university!

What I'm trying to say is that it isn't scientific, and every school is different. As you can see by the chart below.

When I get a call from my clients letting me know they've just gotten an award letter and there's a big grant in there, I know we picked the right school. Getting an award of $30,000 or $40,000 for my clients is amazing and it totally makes my day. With the information in this chapter, I hope you will also have that same experience. So, let's delve into this topic a bit more, so you can fully understand scholarships and grants, and how to position your student to get the most financial aid, so you can get a significant portion of your student's college tuition for free.

What are Scholarships and Grants?

According to IRS Publication 970:

"A scholarship or grant is generally an amount of money paid to a college or given to the student to pay for the pursuit of an education. The student may be either an undergraduate or a graduate."

The first resources that families tend to pursue is scholarships and grants. However, very few parents understand not only how to qualify for scholarships and grants, they also have limited knowledge on how scholarships and grants actually work.

Millions of families want, and many depend on, scholarships and grants to help fund their children's college education. As a result, most parents are told to complete the FAFSA to potentially qualify for Need-Based Aid which includes scholarships and grants from the Federal and State governments, as well as from colleges and universities.

Scholarships are generally paid to the college and used for educational expenses incurred by the student when attending school; however, some scholarships can be used to pay for the students' personal expenses during his or her undergraduate or graduate studies.

Many taxpayers assume that all scholarships and grants are always tax-free. Another assumption is that these funds are defined in the same way by the college and the IRS. This is not true.

Colleges and universities define scholarships and grants as funds that are used for the benefit of the student based on the *need* of the student or on his or her *merit*. The IRS, on the other hand, defines scholarships and grants as qualified, non-qualified, restrictive, or nonrestrictive. The IRS does not care whether the scholarship or grant was given to the student based on need or merit; however, all the IRS is concerned about is how the scholarship or grant is to be used. If the scholarship or grant is used to pay for qualified educational expenses, the scholarship or grant is tax-free to the student. If the funds are used to pay for non-qualified expenses, the scholarship or grant is taxable to the student.

Scholarships can be given out to students based on several financial and non-financial reasons. Most scholarships that are received by students have no repayment requirement to the donor, regardless if the student graduates or drops out before graduating.

The only exception to this rule is, if the scholarship is tied to future or present work obligation to the donor, the student must then claim the scholarship as taxable income in the year it is received. If the student does not work for the donor after graduation, then the scholarship must be repaid with or without interest. In other words, the IRS looks at these types of scholarships as present or future compensation due to the required work or repayment obligations.

A good example of this type of scholarship is when a hospital gives money to the college or university for a particular student that is pursuing a nursing associate or graduate degree. The hospital may require the student to sign an employment agreement to work at the hospital once the student receives their diploma.

Another example is when a student attends a military academy. Since graduates from our military academies must serve in the military forces, the IRS deems the payments for the student's education to be looked upon as future employment compensation.

Academic scholarships are given out mainly based on the high academic achievement of the student. Merit scholarships are normally given to the student based on athletic, artistic, extracurricular activity, or academic achievement of the student. However, many merit scholarships do not require high academic achievements.

In order to receive merit based scholarships from many colleges and universities, the student may need to show more than just high academic achievement. Many colleges may require the student to receive an honorary title or be a scholarship awardee from highly recognized organizations and societies, such as National Merit Scholarships or the National Council of Teachers of English awards.

However, there are also many colleges that will simply require the student to get a certain score on the ACT or SAT and to graduate in the top percentile of their high school class.

Keep in mind most state-supported colleges and universities have limited funds to give to students. Therefore, don't expect large academic scholarships for high academic students. However, since most private colleges and universities charge more than state-supported institutions, they have the ability to give out more merit-based scholarships to their attending students.

Most of the merit scholarships given out by private colleges and universities are actually classified as a discount toward the total cost of attending, even though the college may place a name on the scholarship funds, i.e., XYZ Academic Scholarship.

Now let's look at some of the resources that are available that give college scholarships and grants:

Sources of Scholarships and Grants

Most scholarships are given out from the following resources:

- Federal and State governments
- Colleges and Universities
- Nonprofit and for-profit organizations (which are called outside resources)

Federal and State governments. These entities will generally distribute college funds based solely on the financial need of the student. To qualify for this money, the student must complete the Free Application For Federal Student Aid, better known as the FAFSA.

Colleges, universities, nonprofits, and for-profit organizations give out scholarships based on the need and/or unique talents of the student. That means, the student may have to complete another application other than the FAFSA to receive these dollars.

Always keep in mind, to qualify for Federal and State grants, the student must show financial need for the funds. In other words, most of the Federal and State grants are given out to the neediest students or families. Most of these grants are not given out based on the academic success of the student or the unique talent that the student may have achieved.

HOW TO POSITION YOUR STUDENT TO RECEIVE SCHOLARSHIPS NOT BASED ON NEED

Is Your Student an Attractive Candidate?

As I said earlier, smart college planning requires both choosing the right schools, and qualifying the student for aid. Let's look at a few ideas that college-bound families can use to increase the potential of their students receiving these funds.

Here are a few that all parents should consider:

- **GPA** - Keep the student's GPA above 3.0 (taking advanced courses when available) all the way through high school.

- **Get Involved** - Students should get involved in extra-curricular activities in and out of the high school environment.
- **Get Organized** - Learning organizational skills will make studying and learning much easier.
- **Start Looking Early** - Students should start looking at potential colleges as early as the Sophomore year in high school. Things to consider are academic programs, social, atmosphere, location, student body, etc. In other words, select colleges that are the right fit for the student.
- **ACT/SAT** - Scoring high on either of these two tests are essential when it comes to getting admitted to the student's selected college, as well as positioning the student for scholarships.
- **Search For College Scholarships and Apply** - the best resource for obtaining a list of organizations that give out scholarships is from the high school guidance counselor. Scholarship search should begin in the Sophomore year of high school or no later than the Junior year.

Now that you understand the general make-up of what traditional scholarships and grants are, let's take a twist in a different direction.

WHAT IS A MORAL OBLIGATION SCHOLARSHIP?

There is a hybrid-type scholarship that is being used by several colleges across the country called a Moral Obligation Scholarship.

So how does this hybrid scholarship work?

Any donor (a non-profit organization), college, or university can give out a Moral Obligation Scholarship. The scholarship can impose on the student special restrictions and requirements to receive the funds. The scholarship could require a certain GPA or ACT/SAT test scores, require a financial need or no need, and any other restrictions that the donor or college may feel is important.

When the scholarship is issued, the student will be notified that the scholarship is a Moral Obligation Scholarship. In the notification, it will inform the student that the scholarship has a moral obligation to be **repaid** back to the donor or college once the student has gained employment after graduation.

Generally, the student (upon graduating) will receive a letter from the donor or university informing the student of the amount of funds that was given to them during their stay in college and will request the scholarship to be repaid.

The letter could request the scholarship to be paid in full, or the donor or college could agree on monthly, quarterly, semi-annual, or annual payments over a determined time period.

Now, here is where it gets really interesting.

A Moral Obligation Scholarship is NOT an actual scholarship NOR is it a legal binding debt obligation. It could be looked upon as a gift of funds with a moral obligation to be repaid. Since the scholarship carries a moral obligation of repayment, the student can elect to repay the scholarship, or they can choose to ignore the donor and college's request and pay nothing.

If the student chooses not to repay the scholarship, the donor or college does not have a legal claim for the repayment, because the scholarship has a moral obligation clause within the scholarship agreement.

If the student elects to repay the scholarship, any payment or payments made to the donor (a non-profit organization) or college could be looked upon as a charitable contribution and 100 percent tax deductible as long as the student can complete an IRS Schedule A (itemized deductions).

Now, let's look at some of the moral obligation scholarships that are being given out by colleges and donors that are connected to a college.

Darrell S. Larson Education Scholarship

The purpose of the Darrell S. Larson Education Scholarship will be to assist a student financially in his/her Junior and/or Senior year. The student must be majoring in Elementary Education or Early Childhood Education (Grades 2-8). The student must be in good academic standing and demonstrate financial need. Preferably, the student should be an undergraduate, but the Selection Committee may award the scholarship to a graduate student in Education.

It is the desire of the benefactor that the recipients intend to teach in an elementary or middle school for at least two years after graduation. The recipient should consider this a moral obligation scholarship and should be repaid if the student does not teach for at least two years after graduation.

University of Michigan Scholarships

In keeping with the University's practice and policy, financial assistance is available to qualified students irrespective of sex, race, color, or creed. Scholarships are established by gifts to the College and by allocations from the University's general fund. The loyal alumni and many friends of the University and the College of Engineering—along with other interested individuals, industry, and many public and private organizations—contribute support through annual gifts and endowment funds that earn income to be used for scholarships. There is no direct obligation to repay a scholarship, but recipients recognize their moral obligation to return gifts to the College scholarship fund, according to their abilities, so that other worthy students will benefit.

Dyson Moral Obligation Scholarships, Pace University

These undergraduate and graduate scholarships were established by the late Dr. Charles H. Dyson, '30, former chairman of the Pace University Board of Trustees. The Moral Obligation Scholarship program is based on the idea that students receiving scholarship support from the University incur a moral obligation to replenish the University's scholarship fund in the future. Each generation of scholarship recipients will have the responsibility to provide at least equivalent assistance to future generations of Pace students. Replenishment of the fund, in the form of a tax-deductible donation, is generally expected over a five to ten-year period following graduation. Awards from this fund are restricted to students studying in the Dyson College of Arts and Sciences. Scholarship amounts vary from $500 to full tuition and fees each year, depending on the financial need and academic record of each applicant.

Boston College Law School

The Public Service Scholarships and Robert Drinan, S. J. Scholarship provides scholarships to highly qualified applicants who plan to practice law in the service of the public. In keeping with Boston College Law School's mission of education for the service of others, this program encourages students to seek careers in the public sector, notwithstanding the expense and associated debts of their legal education and the low salaries associated with such careers. Should recipients not pursue careers in public interest law, they must undertake a moral obligation to repay the scholarship fund for at least as much as the value of the scholarship.

The scholarships are renewable annually for three years of study at the law schools.

Financial need, as demonstrated on the Need Access or profile application, will be used to differentiate among otherwise qualified finalists.

After notification of the awards, but before funds are disbursed, Public Service Scholarship recipients must sign a statement acknowledging their intention to enter a career in public service law and their moral obligation to repay Boston College Law School if they do not choose a public service career for a predetermined period of time.

Recipients must reapply each year for the award. The committee will ask for an updated resume and list of activities and summer work (either paid or volunteer) that demonstrates the recipient's continued commitment to the public interest and public service law. Public Service Scholars will be required to provide new commitment letters each year as described above.

** The Public Service Scholarships are 2/3 tuition annually; the Drinan Scholarship is for $6,000 a year.*

Fred and Kit Bigony "Pay-it-Forward" Scholarship Program, Florida Atlantic University

This scholarship support provides "*interest-free loans*" to support students at the Harriet L. Wilkes Honors College at the John D. MacArthur Campus of Florida Atlantic University. The benefactors are providing this support to students who accept the moral obligation to, sometime during their lifetime, "give-back" the support that they have received to support future Wilkes Honors College students further. There is no legal requirement to pay back the funds, but a moral obligation to "pay it forward."

Eligibility Recipients:

- Must be registered full-time at the Harriet L. Wilkes Honors College;
- Must be at the Sophomore level or higher;
- Must demonstrate financial need as determined by their EFC (expected family contribution) as calculated based on a current FAFSA;
- Must be a Florida resident;
- Must be in good standing with a minimum GPA of 3.0;

- Must agree to undertake the moral obligation to make every effort to repay the money received from the Bigony "Pay it Forward" Scholarship—in their lifetime—to benefit future students of the Wilkes Honors College.

Funds may be used to cover costs of tuition, room, and board at an amount up to $5,000 per year. The awards may be renewable up to two additional years to eligible students depending upon available funding. This award will be in addition to a student's Honors College Merit Scholarship.

To conclude this section, I will say that many universities and states are having serious financial problems nationwide. If more colleges and other non-profit organizations would consider applying a moral obligation to the college scholarships, they could potentially recoup thousands of dollars in scholarship monies that could help with their operating expenses or to help future students in obtaining their degrees.

In the next chapter, we will be exploring assessing your student to help find the right fit for their college education, how to apply to multiple colleges, conduct a scholarship search, and the steps to marketing a student athlete. As you'll see, even if you have a highly desirable student, there is still a lot of competition out there. The information in the following chapter is designed to give your child as much of an advantage as possible.

CHAPTER 8

Choosing the Right College

One day, early in my career, I received a phone call from a prospective client who was looking to meet with an advisor. After a few minutes of speaking with him on the phone, I realized that he lived over fifty miles from our office. As we ended our conversation, I assured him that someone would come out to his place for the meeting later that day.

There were three of us in the office that day, and as soon as I got off the phone, we started debating on who should take the appointment and drive all the way out there. We looked up the address the man gave us and discovered not only was it over an hour's drive away, both ways, this person lived in a trailer park. Suddenly, none of us wanted the appointment.

For a couple of minutes, we stood there looking at each other in silence. Finally, I said, "Fine, okay, I'll go."

I was always taught to follow every lead—and besides, I could use the money.

Reluctantly, I got into my car and made the long drive to where this man lived. When I arrived, I knocked on a surprisingly very nice double wide trailer in a higher end RV park. A few moments later, an older gentleman came to the door and let me inside. We sat in his living room, which was tastefully decorated and quite comfortable. After talking for nearly an hour, I discovered the reason for his call: he had just inherited over $2.5 million from his recently deceased mother, and he needed someone to help him manage all that money.

Regardless to say, I was glad I didn't brush him off. To this day, he continues to be one of my best clients, and it was a good lesson: never judge a book by its cover.

The same goes for colleges, don't be a quick judge. When considering which schools to apply to, you're going to have to take a deeper look at what each college has to offer, and also what your student needs. A cursory glance at their website will not be enough, you have to take the time to do your research and find out what they are really offering. Otherwise, you might take the first offer blindly, or miss a great opportunity simply because the school isn't very well known.

Stay open minded. Don't just say, "Oh, we're going to USC," or "We're going to Michigan State." Those are both great schools, but maybe there's a better fit somewhere else.

An important step is familiarizing yourself with the colleges you're applying to. Too often, I see parents get a brochure from a school and the campus looks beautiful, and they fall in love with it. Meanwhile, the photo is just one little corner of the campus, and the rest looks like a dump. Then your child gets there and, before you know it, you get that late night call from he/she, who is miserable and begging to transfer to another school.

This is why I always recommend that parents tour the campus with their student, when possible. Somewhere along this final leg of the process, families inevitably find a school that's a perfect fit and say, "I want to go here!" They also find a lot of other schools that they don't like. The point is they've arrived at a place where they can now make an informed choice, confident in their knowledge that it is the correct one for both their family, their future, and their student's future.

What I'm trying to say is, don't judge a book by its cover. It's hard to believe, but often dinky no-name towns have great liberal arts colleges with amazing programs in them, and they give generously. Most of these lesser known schools are in beautiful college towns, not the boonies. If it's going to reduce your college costs and give your child the education they need to get a great paying job after graduation, it could be well worth it. And just remember, it's only four years.

So, that being said, how do we begin our college search?

College Search

When searching for schools, the first thing you need to consider is the student. The most important element is obviously their grades and test scores, then their career profile, and their interests and hobbies. Sure, grade point average is important, but what are their interests? Do they have a passion for animals? Enjoy winter sports? Musical theater?

The key is to match up your student with the schools that allow them to enjoy their hobbies, in addition to their traditional studies. Then, sort the matches by which schools historically give the most grants and financial aid to students, year after year.

I have included a list of the top two hundred fifty schools ranked by their generosity score. To give you an idea, this is the percentage of the total costs the school will meet in aid (for instance, West Point is 100 percent, meaning they cover all the costs). Every school will have a different generosity score, but this list will give you an idea of which colleges are the most generous when it comes to financial aid. Having this crucial information during your research should significantly help before making your final decision. I recommend you do this before applying to the colleges, so you don't get sticker shock. This way you will know what to expect well in advance.

U.S. College & University Generosity List

Below is the list of the top 250 colleges & universities in the United States, ranked by need-based Generosity.

This list is subject to change.

School Name	City	State	Gen Rank
United States Military Academy	West Point	NY	100
Pomona College	Claremont	CA	99
Amherst College	Amherst	MA	98
Colgate University	Hamilton	NY	97
Vassar College	Poughkeepsie	NY	97
Vanderbilt University	Nashville	TN	96
Yale University	New Haven	CT	96
Claremont McKenna College	Claremont	CA	96
Haverford College	Haverford	PA	96
Swarthmore College	Swarthmore	PA	96
Stanford University	Stanford	CA	95
Columbia University	New York	NY	95
Wellesley College	Wellesley	MA	95
Williams College	Williamston	MA	95
Washington and Lee University	Lexington	VA	94
Harvard University	Cambridge	MA	93
Princeton University	Princeton	NJ	93
Tufts University	Medford	MA	93
Barnard College	New York	NY	93
Hamilton College	Clinton	NY	93
Davidson College	Davidson	NC	93
University of Illinois Chicago	Chicago	IL	92
Rice University	Houston	TX	92
Smith College	Northhampton	MA	92
University of Richmond	Richmond	VA	92
California Institute of Technology	Pasadena	CA	91
Cornell University	Ithaca	NY	91
Middlebury College	Middlebury	VT	91
Washington University in St. Louis	St. Louis	MO	91
Skidmore College	Saratoga Springs	NY	91
Union College	Schenectady	NY	91
University of Chicago	Chicago	IL	90
Duke University	Durham	NC	90
Dartmouth College	Hanover	NH	90
Bates College	Lewiston	ME	90
Macalester College	St. Paul	MN	90
Trinity College	Hartford	CT	90

School Name	City	State	Gen Rank
Mount Holyoke College	South Hadley	MA	89
Brown University	Providence	RI	88
University of Notre Dame	South Bend	IN	88
Occidental College	Los Angeles	CA	88
Bowdoin College	Brunswick	ME	88
Carlton College	Northfield	MN	88
Kenyon College	Gambier	OH	88
Oberlin College	Oberlin	OH	88
Northwestern University	Evanston	IL	87
Bryn Mawr College	Bryn Mawr	PA	87
Brandeis University	Waltham	MA	86
St. Olaf College	Northfield	MN	86
Babson College	Babson Park	MA	86
Denison University	Granville	OH	86
Connecticut College	New London	CT	86
Wesleyan University	Middletown	CT	86
Franklin & Marshall College	Lancaster	PA	86
Wake Forest University	Winston-Salem	NC	85
Pitzer College	Claremont	CA	85
Tulane University	New Orleans	LA	84
Bentley University	Waltham	MA	84
Clark University	Worchester	MA	84
College of Holy Cross	Worchester	MA	84
Harvye Mudd College	Claremont	CA	84
Emory University	Atlanta	GA	83
University of Southern California	Los Angeles	CA	83
Washington College	Chestertown	MD	83
Lafayette College	Easton	PA	83
Sewanee: The University of the South	Sewanee	TN	83
Cornell College	Mount Vernon	IA	82
Loyola University Maryland	Baltimore	MD	82
Gustavus Adolphos College	St. Peter	MN	82
Scripps Research Institute	La Jolla	CA	81
Boston College	Chestnut Hill	MA	81
College of the Ozarks	Point Lookout	MO	81
Baldwin-Wallace University	Berea	OH	81
Scripps University	Claremont	CA	81
Michigan Technological University	Houghton	MI	80
Georgetown University	Washington D.C.	DC	80
University of Pikeville	Pikeville	KY	80
Sarah Lawrence College	Bronxville	NY	80
College of Mount St. Joseph	Cincinnati	OH	80
Dickinson College	Carlisle	PA	80

School Name	City	State	Gen Rank
Grinnell College	Grinnell	IA	89
Mount Holyoke College	South Hadley	MA	89
Brown University	Providence	RI	88
University of Notre Dame	South Bend	IN	88
Occidental College	Los Angeles	CA	88
Bowdoin College	Brunswick	ME	88
Carlton College	Northfield	MN	88
Kenyon College	Gambier	OH	88
Oberlin College	Oberlin	OH	88
Northwestern University	Evanston	IL	87
Bryn Mawr College	Bryn Mawr	PA	87
Brandeis University	Waltham	MA	86
St. Olaf College	Northfield	MN	86
Babson College	Babson Park	MA	86
Denison University	Granville	OH	86
Connecticut College	New London	CT	86
Wesleyan University	Middletown	CT	86
Franklin & Marshall College	Lancaster	PA	86
Wake Forest University	Winston-Salem	NC	85
Pitzer College	Claremont	CA	85
Tulane University	New Orleans	LA	84
Bentley University	Waltham	MA	84
Clark University	Worchester	MA	84
College of Holy Cross	Worchester	MA	84
Harvye Mudd College	Claremont	CA	84
Emory University	Atlanta	GA	83
University of Southern California	Los Angeles	CA	83
Washington College	Chestertown	MD	83
Lafayette College	Easton	PA	83
Sewanee: The University of the South	Sewanee	TN	83
Cornell College	Mount Vernon	IA	82
Loyola University Maryland	Baltimore	MD	82
Gustavus Adolphos College	St. Peter	MN	82
Scripps Research Institute	La Jolla	CA	81
Boston College	Chestnut Hill	MA	81
College of the Ozarks	Point Lookout	MO	81
Baldwin-Wallace University	Berea	OH	81
Scripps University	Claremont	CA	81
Michigan Technological University	Houghton	MI	80
Georgetown University	Washington D.C.	DC	80
University of Pikeville	Pikeville	KY	80
Sarah Lawrence College	Bronxville	NY	80
College of Mount St. Joseph	Cincinnati	OH	80
Dickinson College	Carlisle	PA	80

Now, what about school size?

There are many things to consider, for instance, will your student perform better at a school with 15,000 students, or in smaller sized classes?

School size is also important when considering what your student wants to major in. Some students have no idea what they want to do in life, or worse, they've chosen a dubious major, and you're convinced they're going to change it once they get in there. Sending them to a larger university will allow them to change their major more easily without having to transfer to a smaller college later on. On the other hand, a student who knows exactly what field they want to enter after college, can be sent to either a large state school, or a small university.

Understanding what career the student is interested in will also help narrow down your search quite a bit. I suggest you sit down with your student and have them look at this list of the 100 Best Jobs. Does he/she want to be an engineer? What kind of engineer? Chemical engineering? Aerospace? Is it in high demand?

100 BEST JOBS OF 2020

1. Software Developer
2. Dentist
3. Physician Assistant
4. Orthodontist
5. Nurse Practitioner
6. Statistician
7. Physician
8. Speech-Language Pathologist
9. Oral and Maxillofacial Surgeon
10. Veterinarian
11. Medical and Health Services Manager
12. IT Manager
13. Registered Nurse
14. Mathematician
15. Physical Therapist
16. Optometrist
17. Anesthesiologist
18. Obstetrician and Gynecologist
19. Surgeon
20. Operations Research Analyst
21. Nurse Anesthetist
22. Pediatrician
23. Web Developer
24. Dental Hygienist
25. Genetic Counselor
26. Physical Therapist Assistant
27. Financial Manager
28. Occupational Therapist
29. Psychologist
30. Database Administrator
31. Financial Advisor
32. Mechanical Engineer
33. Civil Engineer
34. Psychiatrist
35. Substance Abuse and Behavioral Disorder Counselor
36. School Psychologist
37. Home Health Aide
38. Information Security Analyst
39. Pilot
40. Respiratory Therapist
41. Diagnostic Medical Sonographer
42. Accountant
43. Market Research Analyst
44. Business Operations Manager
45. Marketing Manager
46. Industrial Psychologist
47. Podiatrist
48. Environmental Engineer
49. Social and Community Service Manager
50. Lawyer

51. Marriage and Family Therapist
52. Medical Assistant
53. Computer Systems Analyst
54. Actuary
55. Medical Records Technician
56. Prosthodontist
57. Construction Manager
58. Veterinary Technologist and Technician
59. Landscaper and Groundskeeper
60. Computer Network Architect
61. Orthotist and Prosthetist
62. Personal Care Aide
63. Computer Systems Administrator
64. Massage Therapist
65. Cartographer
66. Dental Assistant
67. Management Analyst
68. Solar Photovoltaic Installer
69. Physical Therapist Aide
70. Occupational Therapy Assistant
71. Mental Health Counselor
72. Environmental Engineering Technician
73. Nail Technician
74. Plumber
75. Radiologic technologist
76. MRI Technologist
77. Chiropractor
78. Cost Estimator
79. Financial Analyst
80. Insurance Sales Agent
81. School Counselor
82. Nurse Midwife
83. Paralegal
84. Phlebotomist
85. Loan Officer
86. Clinical Social Worker
87. Compliance Officer
88. Dietitian and Nutritionist
89. Ophthalmic Medical Technician
90. Clinical Laboratory Technician
91. Licensed Practical and Licensed Vocational Nurse
92. Electrician
93. HR Specialist
94. Wind Turbine Technician
95. Logistician
96. Residential Advisor
97. Optician
98. Computer Support Specialist
99. Esthetician and Skincare Specialist
100. Restaurant Cook

[Source: https://money.usnews.com/careers/best-jobs/rankings/the-100-best-jobs]

Now, which schools are the top in the nation for that field of study?

The closer you get to understanding what direction your student is headed in, and what their hobbies and interests are, the easier it will be to help guide them toward the school that best matches their ambitions.

I will be addressing SAT and ACT test scores, as well as marketing your student athlete later in the chapter. But first, let's tackle a question I hear a lot from my clients. Does it matter which college you go to?

DO EMPLOYERS REALLY CARE WHERE YOU GET YOUR DEGREE?

Many parents today believe that if their student receives their degree from a prestigious university, they will be able to snag a high paying job after college. In the past, this way of thinking might have been true, however today, graduating from an elite college or university doesn't carry the same weight.

A recent Gallup survey found that hiring managers are far less concerned about what college the student attended or what major the student pursued than you'd think. According to the survey, business leaders are really looking at the skill level and the knowledge a potential candidate has in their field.

The chart below outlines what employers actually find important when looking at hiring new employees.

For Business Leaders: Please tell me if each of the following factors are very important, not very important, or not at all mportant to managers making hiring decisions for organizations. How about...?

	% Very important	% Somewhat important	% Not very important	% Not at all important
Amount of knowledge the candidate has in the field	84	14	2	0
Candidate's applied skills in the field	79	16	2	2
Candidate's college or university major	28	42	22	8
Where the candidate received his or her college degree	9	37	40	14

* Source: 2013 Gallup-Lumina Foundation Business Leaders Poll on Higher Education

Judging by the information gathered in this survey, knowledge and applied skills that are relevant to the business are the two most important factors when hiring new employees. Also, notice the two lowest concerns of potential employers are what college the student attended and what degree they obtained.

According to the Gallup survey, about eight in ten adults working in a business environment agree that knowledge and applied skills in any particular field is most important to managers making hiring decisions for their company.

However, the survey also found the average American still believes the major and where the student received their degree is the most important when it comes to employment. The survey found that nearly half (47 percent) of future employees believe their degree was the most important thing business leaders were looking at, and 30 percent believed where they attended college was very important as well.

According to this survey, business leaders are not downplaying the value of obtaining a college degree. However, they aren't placing nearly as much importance on where a future employee received their degree, or what major they obtained. In other words, business leaders are saying a college degree *alone* is not enough to obtain employment.

The Gallup survey states, "Getting a job and achieving long term success in one's career may increasingly depend on demonstrating real value to employers through **experience** and **targeted learning**—and increasingly less on degrees, **even if they are from prestigious universities**. Higher education institutions have a tremendous opportunity to partner with businesses to bring relevant, responsive, and timely learning opportunities to workplaces in this country and worldwide."

It's clear that business leaders are placing more emphasis on what potential employees **know** and their **style of working**, rather than on the candidate's degree or where they went to college. Keep this in mind while you are searching for colleges for your student to apply to. I always urge parents to consider all their options carefully before investing money into their children's education, and not to get hung up on the idea that an Ivy League degree will be a sure-fire guarantee of success.

Next, let's look at something that is actually important to factor in while searching for colleges: your student's ACT and SAT test scores. The next section will help you figure out which test your student should be focusing on when preparing to apply to colleges.

COMPARING THE ACT AND SAT TEST

In this section, we'll be discussing the differences between the ACT and SAT tests, so you can decide which one your student should take, based on their strengths and weaknesses.

WHAT'S THE NATIONAL AVERAGE ACT SCORE?

According to the American College Test service nearly two million students nationwide took the ACT in 2017/18—1.91 million, to be precise. Out of all of those tests, the national average scores came out as follows:

ACT Section	Average Score
English	20.2
Math	20.5
Reading	21.3
Science	20.7
Composite	**20.8**

WHAT'S THE NATIONAL AVERAGE SAT SCORE?

According to the **College Board's 2018 total group report**, the national SAT average scores (for all 2018 high school graduates) are as follows:

Evidence-Based Reading and Writing:	536
Math:	531
Total Composite	**1068**

On the next few pages, I will outline some of the differences between the two tests that can help you decide which test your student should take to position themselves favorably for top colleges.

For most students, the ACT and SAT are similar, but different. The ACT gives students less time per question so students who need extra time may find the ACT slightly more difficult than the SAT. On the other hand, SAT questions tend to be trickier and the SAT also tests vocabulary indirectly through the **Sentence Completion** questions on the **Critical Reading** section, so certain students may find the ACT easier.

Some test preparation companies have made exaggerated claims that one test favors students of one gender over the other. However, these claims have not been empirically proven and there is no supporting scientific data available. The differences between the two tests are minimal, and ideally, individual students should try both exams to see in which they perform better.

HOW DO THE SAT AND ACT COMPARE?

* The following Charts are Provided By The ACT Testing Service

✓ Yes ✓* Yes for the new SAT test ✗ No

	ACT	SAT
Accepted at all U.S. Colleges	✓	✓
Calculator allowed for entire math test	✓	✗
Essay is optional	✓	✓
No penalty for guessing	✓	✓*
Free daily practice questions	✓	✓
Free comprehensive test practice	✓	✓
Test fees waived for eligible students	✓	✓
Free waiver students eligible for college application fee waiver	✓	✓
Free score reports	✓	✓
All test 1 hour or less	✓	✗
Measures what students learn in high school	✓	✓*
Students always know which questions count	✓	✗
Testing Time	2 hours 55 minutes + 40 minute essay which is optional	3 hours
Structure	4 tests + optional writing test	3 tests + optional essay
Longest Test	1 hour	1 hour 20 minutes
Shortest Test	35 minutes	35 minutes
Score Range	Composite 1-36 (writing domain score 2-12)	Composite 400-1600 (SAT essay reported in 3 dimensions each 2-8)
Measures	What student learns in high school Predicts how student will perform in college	What student learns in high school What student needs to succeed in college

*The following Charts are Provided By The ACT Testing Service

	ACT	**SAT**
Testing Time	2 hours 55 minutes + 40 minute essay which is optional	3 hours
Structure	4 tests + optional writing test	3 tests + optional essay
Longest Test	1 hour	1 hour 20 minutes
Shortest Test	35 minute	35 minutes
Score Range	Composite 1-36 (writing domain score 2-12)	Composite 400-1600 (SAT essay reported in 3 dimensions each 2-8)
Measures	What student learns In high school Predicts how student will perform in college	What student learns in high school What student need to succeed in college

Now that you know the differences between the two tests, let's look at how colleges convert the test scores when the college prefers one test over the other. On the next page, you will see a conversion chart comparing the two tests.

HOW COLLEGES CONVERT SCORES BETWEEN THE SAT AND ACT

SAT	ACT	SAT	ACT	SAT	ACT
1600	36	1250	26	900	17
1590	35	1240	26	890	16
1580	35	1230	25	880	16
1570	35	1220	25	870	16
1560	35	1210	25	860	16
1550	34	1200	25	850	15
1540	34	1190	24	840	15
1530	34	1180	24	830	15
1520	34	1170	24	820	15
1510	33	1160	24	810	15
1500	33	1150	23	800	14
1490	33	1140	23	790	14
1480	32	1130	23	780	14
1470	32	1120	22	770	14
1460	32	1110	22	760	14
1450	32	1100	22	750	13
1440	31	1090	21	740	13
1430	31	1080	21	730	13
1420	31	1070	21	720	13
1410	30	1060	21	710	12
1400	30	1050	20	700	12
1390	30	1040	20	690	12
1380	29	1030	20	680	12
1370	29	1020	20	670	12
1360	29	1010	19	660	12
1350	29	1000	19	650	12
1340	28	990	19	640	12
1330	28	980	19	630	12
1320	28	970	18	620	11
1310	28	960	18	610	11
1300	27	950	18	600	11
1290	27	940	18	590	11
1280	27	930	17	580	11
1270	26	920	17	570	11
1260	26	910	17	560	11

* Source: The College Board

HOW IMPORTANT ARE THE ACT AND SAT TEST SCORES?

The SAT and ACT still remain two of the most important factors colleges look at when considering a potential student. There are two reasons why students should have as high a test score as possible.

- **Admission to Top Colleges**
- **Scholarship Money**

Admission to Top Colleges: When applying for college enrollment, colleges and universities (especially private), will use the test scores to determine the admission potential of the student. The higher the test scores the higher the potential of being admitted. Many colleges also use the test scores to determine if the student needs to take prerequisite courses. Prerequisite courses are course studies that need to be taken by the student in order to bring their knowledge of the subject matter up to a college level. Keep in mind, many times, these required courses **will not** count toward the student's degree.

Scholarship Money: Most students want to receive as much scholarship money as possible. The ACT or SAT test scores can increase or decrease your student's potential of getting merit-based scholarship money. Colleges (especially private), will reward students with high ACT or SAT test scores with scholarship money. Colleges are willing to invest in students that are of high-quality academically.

Scholarships that are given out by many **outside resources** will use a combination of the student's GPA and ACT or SAT test scores to give their scholarships funds out as well.

Lastly, most students that have high ACT or SAT test scores will graduate on time (four years), which could affect the amount of money the family will have to spend on their education. According to the College Board, the average time (nationwide) of getting an undergraduate degree is around 5.6 years. If you look at the cost of a college education today, this could amount to several **thousands** of dollars.

Important Development:

An **Adversity Score** has been added to the SAT in recent years. The additional score is intended to measure the hardships that high school students have faced in their lives prior to applying to college.

According to the College Board, "The adversity score, which will be shared with colleges and universities along with a student's SAT performance is based on 31 data points that, according to research, are correlated with academic achievement. They include factors associated with an applicant's neighborhood (such as the percentage of adults with less than a high school diploma) and those tied to a student's high school (such as the number of Advanced Placement courses offered). College admissions officers are already placing great weight on the measure."

A study in the *Harvard Educational Review* said, "The pre-screening of questions on the verbal portion of the exam favors the inclusion of items that generate larger white-black disparities. This finding is backed up by other research indicating that standardized test scores underestimate minority academic achievement."

So, please keep all these factors in mind—SAT and ACT scores, adversity scores, and positioning your student accordingly—as you continue to search for the best college to attend.

Now, let's address applying to colleges when dealing with a student who has high athletic potential.

THE FIVE STEPS OF MARKETING A STUDENT ATHLETE:

1. Become proactive in the marketing process

Many families assume that college coaches will hear about their student athlete from their high school or summer league coaches. Hoping that newspaper clippings from the local paper will be enough exposure to get the student athlete discovered and recruited. This is far from true.

The marketing process is the student athlete's responsibility and no one else.

2. Find the right academic program

Most student athletes go to college just to play sports—they don't really give much thought to academics. When this occurs, though, the athlete often overlooks the right fit regarding their academic studies, and in many cases, athletically as well. In reality, you want to focus on both, as a track record of academic excellence in high school can lead to larger athletic scholarships, and top academic scores in college can lead to better job opportunities after college.

In order to achieve the right balance, student athletes must consider their academic study more important than athletics, which means finding the right academic program comes first, and playing sports comes second.

3. Research college athletic programs

Many student athletes make the mistake of not researching the college or even the athletic program itself before accepting an admission to a college that has offered them an athletic scholarship. Athletes should look at several things before committing to a particular college and athletic program. The athlete should consider the following:

- **Team roster** (will you be able to play quickly, or will you have to wait a few years);
- **The competition** (does it match your athletic ability);

- **Coach's philosophy and playing style** (does it match your philosophy and playing style).

Knowing these things ahead of time will make the college and athletic program selection much easier. It will also eliminate any surprises once you begin the college career.

4. Keep your grades up

Your athletic skills may get the interest of some selective colleges or universities, but grades will dictate your admission chances. The NCAA has minimum academic requirements, but many colleges have much more stringent academic rules and regulations.

While in high school, the student-athlete should excel academically and build strong organizational and study skills. This will help the student once they are in college and will make the transition much easier.

If the student athlete has strong organizational and study skills, it will also help the athlete balance academic requirements and athletic participation.

5. Research other forms of financial aid assistance

All scholarships are identical, regardless of whether the scholarship is based on need, merit, or athletics. Some colleges will substitute an athletic scholarship with an academic scholarship, or another tuition incentive.

This is commonly done in NCAA Division III colleges where there are no athletic awards or in NCAA Division II or NAIA colleges in order to maximize the school's athletic budget.

There is a big difference between need-based and academic-based scholarships when compared to athletic scholarships. The major difference is the athletic scholarship is given or earned each year based mostly on the athletic accomplishments of the student athlete. If the student athlete were to get injured, quits, or does not perform up to the expectation of the college coach, they could lose the scholarship.

Compare this with a need-based or academic-based scholarship. The student athlete who receives these types of scholarships can only lose the award if they do not perform academically or the family's need decreases. These scholarships have **nothing** to do with the student athlete's athletic ability. If the student were to blow out their knee or break their arm, or quits playing intercollegiate athletics altogether, the student would **not** lose a need-based or academic-based scholarship, unless they fall below the academic standards or the family's need decreases.

Money is money, regardless of what form it comes in—and it is always better to have options.

Speaking of money, in the next chapter we will be preparing you for paying for college, calculating your estimated family contribution, student loans, and all the hidden costs associated with college that nobody thinks about.

CHAPTER 9

Paying for College

On any given day, a couple walks into my office and sits down in the chairs across from my desk. We begin our college planning session with a few simple questions.

The first thing I ask them is: "Before you came here today, how were you planning on paying for college?"

The husband and wife look at each other.

Most of my clients will answer this question with, "We're hoping for student loans," or "We have some savings," or sometimes they will just say, "We have no idea, that's why we're here."

"That's okay," I tell them. "We're going to figure this out before you leave today."

Living Pay Check to Pay Check?

- Savings?
- Borrow?
- Scholarship?
- Go to a lesser school?
- Not go at all?

Now it's my job to inform them of their options. "You could borrow money, you could go paycheck to paycheck, you could find scholarships, you could dip into your savings..."

From there we begin to analyze their financial needs, their level of preparedness, the timeline of events, and ultimately determine—what's best for your situation?

This leads us to the point where I need to classify which type of families they are. I have noticed there are three categories of families:

1. The first are families that no matter what will qualify for need-based financial aid. They are on the lower end of the income scale, but the system works perfectly for them, although they need to choose their schools carefully.

2. The second type is the typical middle class family. They may have a college funding strategy in place and may or may not qualify for need-based financial aid. These families are looking to lower their expected family contribution based on their income and assets.

3. The third group are the upper middle class and wealthy families who will not qualify for need-based aid. If we are able to catch this type of family early enough, they can pay for college on a tax-favored ba-

sis. They also have more financial options available, but their strategies tend to be more complex.

Which one of these families doesn't have to fill out a FAFSA form? None. All of them have to apply for financial aid. Even if you make $1,000,000 plus a year, and your student is a star track runner, you may be in line for an academic or athletic-based scholarship. No school is going to give you that money unless you fill out the FAFSA form. You cannot skip steps in this process, no matter how much money you make.

There's no way around it.

For instance, my niece is a great student and she got an academic grant from The University of Dayton when she applied to college there. Her father makes a lot of money, but that doesn't matter. In order to get that grant scholarship, the school still demanded they fill out the FAFSA paperwork.

As you probably guessed, category 1 families require only the easiest, most straightforward college planning. On the other hand, category 2 and 3 need to be a bit more creative to find financial aid.

So, now let's focus on a couple unique strategies that work for category 2 and 3 families. Two popular strategies are funding 529 plans and Indexed Universal Life Policies (IULs). These two financial vehicles are especially good for early planners, but if your student is already in high school, neither of these may serve your purpose.

That being said, let's examine these two strategies more in depth.

PAYING FOR COLLEGE USING 529 PLANS AND IULS

Paying for a child, or a grandchild's college education has become increasingly tricky, as the costs of college continue to increase, year over year. As a result, 529 plans have become the go-to tool of choice for pre-funding and building a tax-favored pool of money to use toward your student's tuition. A 529 plan is essentially a tax advantaged investment vehicle, sponsored by the state or a state agency.

Here are the pros and cons of 529 plans:

Pros—

1. Once funded (after taxes), the money can grow tax-free and be removed tax-free for qualifying college education expenses.

2. If owned by the parent or grandparent, once funded correctly, the assets including growth are out of their estate for (estate) tax purposes.

3. If owned by the parent or grandparent, if the child or grandchild does not go to college, the money can be used by

the person funding the 529 plan and would act like an IRA (with similar income taxes and penalties).

Cons—

1. If the child or grandchild does not go to college, the growth on the money is taxable and subject to potential penalties when withdrawn/used by the parent or grandparent.

2. The money in a 529 plan is subject to loss due to market risk.

3. 529 plans are not "self-completing" should a parent or grandparent die prior to complete funding.

4. 529 plans have funding limits. Funding is limited by the $13000 annual gift tax exclusion (although they can be super-funded in year one by pouring in all of the first five years' worth of gifts all at once, $65,000).

USING CASH VALUE LIFE INSURANCE TO FUND COLLEGE (IUL)

Why would anyone use cash value life insurance (IUL) as a funding vehicle to pay for college costs? Good question. Here are the simple reasons, assuming that the life insurance policy will be purchased on a child's parent.

1. Life insurance is a "self-completing" plan. Let's assume Dad is the breadwinner in the family; and if he happens to

die when the child is young, without fully funding a 529 plan, there will be a significant shortfall when the child goes to college. With life insurance, if Dad dies, a sizable income tax-free death benefit will be paid to the heirs, who can then choose to use that money for college education.

2. Money in a cash value policy will not only grow tax-free, but it can also be removed tax-free when used to pay for college expenses, in the form of policy loans.

3. If the child does not go to college, the policy will be a terrific tax favorable wealth building retirement tool for the parent.

4. After borrowing from the policy, it will still have cash in it and should continue to grow for years to come. That means that money can be removed tax-free later on when the parent is in retirement (this is not possible with a 529 plan).

5. Money in a cash value life insurance policy is not a countable asset when a child goes to apply for financial aid for college (this is the case with most colleges, but not all).

Based on the above 'pros' of using a cash value life insurance policy, you'd likely assume it's an easy decision in most cases to counsel a client to use this vehicle to fund their student's college education. Unfortunately, that is not the case. As you will see, cash value life insurance as a college funding vehicle only works when a client not only funds the policy for future college expenses, but also **overfunds** the policy with cash to be used as a supplemental retirement vehicle for the parents.

Let's take a look at the problems with using cash value life insurance without overfunding it, and also give some examples to illustrate how an IUL works when used properly.

The key to this model of overfunding is not just about funding the policy at the MEC minimum death benefit, but instead, it's about paying a sizable premium into the policy over a short period of time (ten years or less).

What's sizable? In the college funding scenario, it's funding the policy with not only the amount of money a client can budget for college planning, but also for supplemental retirement planning (income) for the parents. Obviously, not all parents are prepared to do that. Affluent clients simply have the money on hand and only need to choose to allocate it, whereas lower income parents will have to "find" the money first.

So, where can a parent "find" this extra money to fund into the life insurance policy and overfund it?

Two main places:

1. Reallocate money from a 401K plan.

Many clients fund tax deferred 401K plans for retirement savings. While this sounds like a good idea for most clients under the age of fifty, funding cash value life insurance after taxes will be a better, more favorable, and conservative way to grow wealth. Therefore, instead of funding $5,000-$15,000 into a tax deferred qualified plan, the client can allocate that money to funding a cash value life insurance policy. This additional funding will make the life insurance policy work better as a tool to accumulate money and should allow for plenty of extra funding to be used for both college and retirement.

2. Borrow money from a home.

Many clients have a major asset in the equity of their personal residence and will not hesitate to strip equity from their home to send their children to college at the last minute. This is essentially poor planning, though. When done properly, this equity can be used ahead of time to overfund a cash value life insurance policy and significantly increase the financial viability of that vehicle, to use as both a college funding strategy, and a tax-favored retirement vehicle.

In summary, using cash value life insurance from a purely financial standpoint is very difficult to justify for most average clients who are only looking to minimally fund the policy for college planning. But the IUL does have some significant advantages over the 529 plan such as:

- An IUL policy self-completes, providing a back-up plan for a parent who dies.
- An IUL is locking in investment gains every year.

- An IUL allows the client to use the funds tax-free for any other purpose.
- An IUL allows the client to keep the policy in force until he or she retires and potentially borrows more money out of the policy tax-free.
- An IUL isn't a countable asset for financial aid calculations.
- An IUL can also come with significant perks such as a long-term rider to protect the client when in retirement.

When a client is able to properly overfund a cash value life insurance policy, it can be a very powerful financial vehicle, with a high probability of success, in addition to the many other advantages listed above. If you feel either the 529 plan or IUL are suitable strategies for your college planning needs, please speak with an advisor, as these need to be set up by a professional.

FEDERAL WORK-STUDY: ANOTHER WAY TO PAY FOR COLLEGE

Now, let's talk about a strategy that can be used by all three categories of clients, no matter what your income or level of preparedness. Federal work-study.

To qualify for Federal work-study, the student must complete the free application for student aid, and ideally the FAFSA should be filled out as early as possible. The reason why the

FAFSA should be completed sooner rather than later, is that funds are limited, and Federal work-study programs are given out on a first-come-first-serve basis.

Under a Federal work-study, a student can work part-time, and many of the jobs could be located on campus. However, some Federal work-study programs can be off campus as well.

Here are a few things you need to know about Federal work-study:

- **No Guarantees**

If a student qualifies for Federal work-study, there are no guarantees of receiving the funds. When a student receives a financial aid offer, and it includes Federal work-study funds, the student needs to start applying to work positions at the college that are available. It is a good idea to look for job opportunities that go along with the major the student is interested in pursuing. Working is an excellent opportunity for the student to get experience in their field of study. Before the student is offered the job, many colleges will require the student to go through an interview process just like any other job application.

- **Work-Study Jobs May Not Be at the College**

As I mentioned earlier, the job may be on or off the college campus. Many off-campus work-study jobs will include working for nonprofit employers. It could be working for a community elementary or high school or some other community service position. If the student is particularly interested in working with nonprofits, they should check with the financial aid office to see if any of these positions are available.

- **Work-Study Earnings Are Paid Directly to the Student**

Even though a Federal work-study is a form of financial aid, the earnings are not automatically applied toward the student's college expenses. When a student earns money through the Federal work-study, they will be issued a paycheck just like any other job. Federal, state, social security, and local income taxes will be withheld from the student's earnings. However, when completing the FAFSA for the next school year, the student should claim these earnings as an exemption so it will not affect the family's expected contribution (EFC).

- **Work-Study Jobs That Are on Campus May Not Be Available**

Remember, there's no guarantees. Many colleges and universities may not have adequate funds under the Federal work-study program to give to all qualifying students. However, this does not mean the student cannot be employed in a work position that is on campus that needs to be filled. Many colleges try to fill jobs for different departments at the college that don't qualify for Federal work-study funds. A student that is interested in being employed on campus should check with the employment office at the college they are attending.

- **You Are Not Guaranteed Federal Work-Study Funds Year After Year**

Qualifying for Federal work-study funds is from year to year and eligibility for the funds is determined by the information that is submitted on the Free Application for Student Aid (FAFSA) every year. This means the student could receive Federal work-study funds one year and not qualify for the next year.

- **Hourly Wages Could Fluctuate**

The hourly wage that a student can earn under a Federal work-study could vary and is based on the student's qualifications and the type of job that is to be performed. Typically, the college will pay at least the minimum wage requirements that are established in the state that the college is located in.

- **Number of Hours the Student May Work Can Fluctuate**

The number of hours the student can work will be regulated by the employer and the type of job that is to be performed. Sometimes the hours of employment can be scheduled around the student's class schedule. Normally work-study jobs have average work hours of ten to twenty hours per week. However, keep in mind this is not a set rule.

- **Federal Work-Study and Financial Aid Eligibility**

As we had mentioned earlier, earnings from Federal work-study funds will not count against the student when they complete the FAFSA form the next year. There is a question on the FAFSA form that will ask the student if they have earnings through Federal work-study, so make sure to complete this question when applying for financial aid for another school year.

Working while attending college could be a great benefit to the student, especially working in the same field that the student is getting their degree. Not only will it give the student valuable experience, it will also create additional funds that can be used to keep the student debt down to a minimum and relieve some of the parent's expected contribution.

I hope this chapter has given you an idea of the types of options available to you to help you pay for college, outside of student loans, grants, and scholarships. My philosophy has always been to educate parents on the different types of strategies available, to help them find the right combination of methods that will make paying for college less intimidating. Whether you are in category 1, 2, or 3, or whether you are an early planner or a "last minute" type of planner, I truly believe everyone should be able to afford college.

In the next chapter, we will be going through the nitty gritty details of applying for colleges and real college costs, comparing financial award letters, and filling out the FAFSA form properly whether you're single, married, divorced, or separated.

CHAPTER 10

Admissions and Financial Aid Realities

Most families underestimate (or overlook) what it actually costs for their students to attend college. Parents will often rely entirely on college websites where the published total cost of attendance is estimated. However, there are plenty of other costs that can crop up once the student gets to the ivy-covered walls of their selected college or university. So, before we delve into the realities of financial aid, here's some useful information for you, and it's something that never fails to shock families—college expenses that nobody thinks of.

COLLEGE COSTS NOBODY THINKS ABOUT

Cost of Attendance

Tuition and Fees
+ Room and Board
+ Books
+ Transportation
+ Cost of Computer
+ Miscellaneous Expenses

= Cost of Attendance (COA)

According to an article from *The Washington Post*, "The average undergrads spend $765 every year eating off campus, even if their parents have already shelled out for a meal plan. A bus pass to get to an off-campus job or internship can be $50 a month or more. Dorm insurance or renter's insurance might cost a couple of hundred dollars per year."

According to Consumer Reports, "Laundry isn't free. You might pay fees for joining a club or storing personal items over the summer. Concerts, sporting events, and movie nights add up too."

And according to Edvisors, a website that provides information on planning and paying for college, "Unforeseen college costs can add up to an additional $250 to $500 every month. For the unprepared, the extra expenses can be a major financial strain. Sixty-four percent of college students have run out of money before the end of the semester at least once. Unanticipated costs were to blame for drained bank accounts in half of those cases."

Unforeseen or unbudgeted additional college costs could very easily break a family's college budget. So, in the spirit of full disclosure, here is a list of some of the unforeseen college costs that most families overlook:

- Application fees paid to various colleges can total hundreds of dollars
- Taking the SAT (including the essay test) costs $57 - ACT fees are similar

- Advanced Placement exam costs $93 on average
- Fees for the college fitness center - often the fees aren't optional
- Fees for health insurance - often the fees aren't optional
- Dorm room refrigerator rental
- TV cable fees
- Charges for a visit to the college's student health center
- Charges to print a paper for class
- Charges for the cap and gown to wear to college graduation
- Charges for using a credit card
- Once you graduate, you could pay extra charges for copies of your transcripts for graduate school applications
- Additional cost of joining a fraternity or sorority - including formal events, gifts for sorority or fraternity sister or brother, and clothing, etc.
- Annual dues, fines for infractions (like skipping a required meeting)
- Fees for social events, and purchases of T-shirts and other college gear
- Cost of transportation – travel to and back to college
- If student owns a car, they will have to pay campus parking fees
- Students that don't have a car on campus may incur bus pass fees or Uber fares
- Lab fees and instructional materials
- Music or performing arts majors might have to pay extra for practice room time
- Spring breaks to Florida or other warm locations

Adding up all the additional college costs that are overlooked could cost the family several thousands of dollars over their students' stay in college. Therefore, putting together a cash flow and tax plan to cover college costs is so important. These are all very good points to bring up with your college planning advisor during your assessment.

As I mentioned earlier, it's very likely your college planner will walk you through the FAFSA application process, and it's a relatively straightforward process if the student's parents are still married, but it can be tricky for parents who aren't. I have prepared a list of additional questions and information for parents navigating the college planning process who are either divorced or separated, and for students who have guardians other than their biological parents.

FAFSA QUESTIONS PERTAINING TO DIVORCED OR SEPARATED PARENTS:

How Do You Apply for Aid?

Filling Financial Aid Forms

- The FAFSA
- The CSS Profile Form
- Institutional Forms
- Verification Forms
- Additional Forms:
  - Business Supplement
  - Divorce / Separated Agreement

- **If the Parents Are Divorced, Whose Information Should Be Used On The FAFSA?**

According to FAFSA rules, "Normally it is the parent that the student lives with the most during the year. It does not make a difference which parent claims the student as a dependent for tax purposes. If the student doesn't live with either parent or lived equally with each parent, the parental information must be provided for the parent from whom the student receives the most financial support or the parent from whom the student receives the most support the last time support was given."

If the student is a dependent student and their parent (or parents) are remarried, the stepparent's information must be included, or the student will not be considered for Federal Student Financial Aid.

- **If the Parents Are Separated, but NOT Divorced, and the Student Lives with One of the Parents, Which Parent's Income and Assets Does the Student Use When Completing The FAFSA, if the Parents File Joint Tax Returns?**

Report only the parent's income and asset information for whom the student lives with the most during the year or the parent that provides the most support. The parents **do not** have to be **legally** separated. However, they **must** have two separate living addresses that show the parents are not living together. If the parents are separated but still live together, the FAFSA will still consider them married and living together. If the parents live apart and file a joint tax return, use the custodian's **(parent one or parent two's)** W-2 Form or other records to determine the parent's share of the income reported and taxes paid on the tax return. Sometimes you can get this information off the parents' state tax return.

- **How is Income Received for Child Support Treated When Completing the FAFSA?**

According to FAFSA rules, if you are receiving child support from an ex-spouse, you **MUST** report child support you received for **ALL** children. Do not include foster care or adoption payments.

- **The Student Does Not Live With Their Birth Parents and Lives with the Grandparents or Other Individuals. Whose Financial Information Should Be Used to Complete The FAFSA–Their Parents or the Person That the Student Lives With?**

If the person or persons the student lives with have **NOT** legally adopted the student, that person or person's financial information should **NOT** be used in calculating the student's EFC.

If the student is living with another person or persons other than their birth parents and were classified as a ward of the court, the student would only need to put their financial information on the FAFSA, as an independent student. If this is not the case and the whereabouts of the birth parents are known, the student needs to get the birth parents' financial information (whether divorced or separated) and use this income on the FAFSA.

I would recommend getting professional help in dealing with this situation. Talk to the student's guidance counselor, professional college consultant, or call the college that the student will be attending for guidance.

- **If the Parents Are Divorced and One of the Parents Would Benefit More (Qualify for the Educational Tax Credits and Educational Deductions) by Claiming the Student as a Dependent, What Must the Custodial Parent Do in Order to Give the Dependence Exemption to the Other Parent?**

Under IRS Code Sec. 152(e), a noncustodial parent can only claim a dependency deduction for a qualifying child or qualifying relative of the taxpayer if the custodial parent submits a release of claim to the exemption.

A release of a claim to an exemption can only be executed in two ways:

1. *Complete Form 8332, Release/Revocation of Release of Claim to Exemption for Child by Custodial Parent, or successor form; or*

2. *A written declaration that is not on Form 8332 but conforms to the substance of that form and that is a document executed for the sole purpose of releasing the claim.*

Many parents of a college student may feel a court order or decree, or a separation agreement can serve as the written declaration. However, this is not true, according to the IRS, the noncustodial parent must attach a copy of Form 8332 or the written declaration to the parent's return for each year that the child is claimed as a dependent.

Once Form 8332 or written declaration is completed, the noncustodial parent can claim the student as a dependent and potentially qualify for the college tax credits or deductions.

Now that we've covered some of the trickier aspects of applying for financial aid for divorced or separated parents, let's talk about another stressful aspect of college planning: comparing financial aid award letters. This is another area I notice many parents struggling with. In the next section, I lay out some steps that should help you decipher these award letters and get the most out of the colleges you've applied to.

COMPARE FINANCIAL AID AWARD LETTERS

Award Letter

Details of Award

- Grants and Scholarships
- Student Loans
- Word-Study
- Accept, deny, or appeal any portion
- Acceptance will maintain the award

During the fall, many high school Seniors have begun completing their FAFSA forms and waiting for the Student Aid Report (SAR) with their Expected Family Contribution (EFC). Now students are turning all their attention in selecting a college to attend. This can be a very trying time for many students and their parents.

Most students have received acceptance letters from the colleges they have applied to, and many have received financial aid award letters. Now comes the time to evaluate which college to attend and how to interpret the offer of financial assistance from each college.

Understanding how to interpret the financial aid awards can be a daunting task. When comparing the financial aid award letters, you need to pay close attention to the family's total out-of-pocket expense for each college.

It is difficult in many situations to come up with your total out-of-pocket expense because many award letters don't always make this clear to the student. However, there are things that students and their parents can do to narrow down what the college will expect them to pay.

In order to get to the bottom line, here are a few things that are important factors to consider in making sure you are comparing "apples to apples."

Identify the total cost of attending: Total cost of attending includes tuition/fees, room/board, books/supplies, and miscellaneous costs. Sometimes it may consist of activity fees and possibly lab fees. Most award letters will not outline all of these costs. Therefore, it is a good idea to consult with the school's website or school officials for the complete list of the cost that could incur.

Identify all gift aid: Gift aid consists of scholarships and grants. Many times, these funds are given out by the State and Federal governments and the college itself. If the student will receive scholarships from other outside resources such as churches, clubs, and corporations they should include these funds as gift aid.

Subtract all gift aid from the total cost of attending: This will help determine the overall **out-of-pocket expense** for your family.

Now that we have identified the total cost of attending and gift aid awards, we now know our total out-of-pocket expenses to attend each college. The next steps students and parents should take is looking at self-help aid.

Self-help aid: Examples of self-help aid that most colleges will award, include federally-guaranteed student loans, Federal and State work-study, and Parents Loans for Undergraduate Students, **(PLUS).** Students may find each award letter could be identical when offering federally-guaranteed student loans. The only difference in an offer is whether the Federal loan is subsidized or unsubsidized. However, the **amount** of a federally-guaranteed loan should be identical. If the award contains a **PLUS** loan, the loan amount could vary from one college to the other. Another variable from one offered to the next is the amount of Federal and/or State work-study aid.

Be aware of "gapping": Many colleges and universities will not meet 100 percent of the students need. Some may only cover 60 percent to 70 percent and some 90 percent of the need of the student. When this happens, it is called **"gapping."** This practice occurs more often than you may realize. This practice forces the student and parents to find the needed funds from other sources such as nontraditional student loans, forcing the parents to borrow on their home or use more money from the family's spendable income, just to name a few.

Some colleges will advertise that they will meet 100 percent of the student's need. Sometimes this is very misleading. In many situations, a substantial part of the student's remaining need is covered by a Parent Loan for Undergraduate Students, better known as the **PLUS** loan (as we have mentioned earlier).

Once the student knows how much gift and self-help aid each college has offered, they should subtract the offers from the colleges' total cost of attending.

Sometimes students and parents can ask for more financial aid. However, in order for the college to increase the aid package, the family must show some financial hardship that is preventing them from meeting the expected family contribution.

If the parents have a high academic student or have a student with special skills or talents, they could ask for more gift aid and fewer loans. Also, in some situations, if the student is applying to colleges that compete for the same students and some of the colleges offered more gift aid than the students preferred college, they could increase their gift aid award by notifying their preferred college and provide them the other colleges' gift aid award and ask for more free money.

When it's all said and done, it is always a good idea to ask for more gift aid from the college that the student wants to attend. If the college can't or will not revise the financial aid offer, the student will **NOT** be any worse off by asking for more free money than they were before.

Here's the last rule of thumb, before you submit an enrollment deposit, the family must be comfortable with their ability to manage the cost of attending a college. If you have concerns, it is advisable to consult with a professional college consultant that has no ties to the colleges that the student is interested in attending. Also, (as we have mentioned earlier), most college financial aid offices will entertain appeals to their financial offer. This could occur as long as you can provide documentation and concrete reasons why you feel you need more financial assistance.

SOME LAST WORDS OF ADVICE

I suggest that you utilize these techniques I just laid out in this chapter, taking each award letter and applying it to your own financial situation, and comparing each one. This should give you an idea of what is possible for your own student, as well as give you some inspiration, hopefully.

If you take one thing from this book, I hope that you feel a little less overwhelmed about the college planning process. I hope that you understand that college can be affordable, and with an open mind and some creative strategies, you can secure a great education for your student. Finally, I hope that you don't try to scam the system, but get actual professional guidance, and consider all your options before committing to any course of action.

Good luck!

Made in United States
North Haven, CT
04 November 2026

21771548R00099